MW01104322

Rotten to the Core
The Politics of the Manitoba Métis Federation

Rotten *to the* CRE

The Politics
of the
Manitoba
Métis
Federation

by Sheila Jones Morrison

© 1995, Sheila Jones Morrison

All rights reserved. No part of this book may be reproduced, stored in a retrieval system or transmitted in any form or by any means without written permission from 101060, an imprint of J. Gordon Shillingford Publishing Inc., except for brief excerpts used in critical reviews, for any reason, by any means, without the permission of the publisher.

Cover design by Terry Gallagher/Doowah Design
Cover photo used by permission of CBC Manitoba
Author photo by John Tyler

Printed and bound in Canada by Hignell Printing Ltd.

Canadian Cataloguing in Publication Data

Morrison, Sheila Jones, 1954-
Rotten to the core

Includes bibliographical references and index.
ISBN 1-896239-08-0

1. Manitoba Métis Federation. 2. Métis—Manitoba—Politics and government. *
3. Métis—Manitoba—Government relations.
I. Title.
FC126.M3M67 1995   971.27'00497   C95-910562-X
E99.M47M67 1995

*In memory of my father
Harold Jones,
a politician of great integrity.*

ACKNOWLEDGMENTS

One of the biggest obstacles to writing this book was fear. The fear stems from rumours of people who "know" someone who died suspiciously, someone who's teeth were removed with the business end of a baseball bat, someone who's car brake lines were cut.

Fear is contagious, and during the hundreds of hours I spent at people's kitchen tables (once I'd convinced them I wasn't working for one political faction of another) listening to their stories, I wondered if I, too, should be afraid. Some people panicked after interviews, and begged me not to use their names. Even people of some standing in the community agreed to meet with me only after I swore *no one* would ever know they'd talked to me. To all those people who were willing to talk to me, on or off the record, I owe a debt of gratitude. This story could not have been written without your courage to tell the story behind the news headlines.

I'd like to acknowledge the *Winnipeg Free Press* and CBC Winnipeg for the generous access to their research libraries. But my most heart-felt thanks go to my friends Julie Bell, Donna Webb and Allan Webb for their editorial and moral support, and to Gilbert Le Gras for insisting I keep his bullet-proof vest, just in case.

TABLE OF CONTENTS

CHAPTER ONE

THE GLORY DAYS

The heat was on. Brian Mulroney had hitched his political credibility to the success of the Charlottetown Accord. Métis leader Yvon Dumont had a lot tied to the constitutional deal, too. It was the summer of 1992, and the deadline for the national referendum on the Charlottetown Accord was fast approaching, but it was far from a done deal. The Prime Minister's point man on Charlottetown, Joe Clark, had his work cut out for him negotiating support for the Accord with almost every special interest lobby group in the country.

The Manitoba Métis Federation (MMF), led by Yvon Dumont, had already thrown its full support behind the Yes side of the campaign. After all, the Métis National Council (MNC), led by Yvon Dumont, had struck a deal with Mulroney and Clark to make the Métis' inherent right to self-government part of the Canadian constitution. Along with that was a promise from Mulroney himself to build a Métis nation...complete with self-government and a land base. After all, nation-hood status rings hollow if it's not accompanied by constitutional jurisdiction over somebody, somewhere, and guaranteed transfer payments for the governing of the new nation.

The MNC had high expectations—recognition of the Métis as a founding nation of Canada, a land base, self-government, and guaranteed Métis seats in the House of Commons and the reformed Senate. But all that was being negotiated under a parallel Métis accord, to be signed *after* Charlottetown had passed. Dumont was telling the Métis people that they were going to have their own schools, their own legislature, equalization payments from Ottawa, the jurisdiction to enact legislation governing all Métis in the new Métis nation, and the right to decide who would be allowed membership in the new nation.

It was heady stuff. Real power and money. Not just the tens of millions of dollars doled out annually to Métis organizations by the provinces and Ottawa. Not just power under the stifling regulations of the Corporations Act. If Métis people had reservations about the Charlottetown Accord, the idea of a Métis nation (and lots of money to go with it) was tempting. The people who had always had so little were on the verge of getting so much. The Métis organizations in Ontario, Saskatchewan, Alberta, British Columbia and the Northwest Territories were all on side, under the umbrella of the Métis National Council.

Dumont was playing with the big boys. The kid who'd grown up working in his parents' store in the impoverished community of St. Laurent on the shore of Lake Manitoba was rubbing shoulders with the first ministers. He not only had a direct pipeline to the Prime Minister's Office, he had a direct line to the big man himself.

In the months preceding the national referendum on the Charlottetown Accord, few Canadians could escape being pulled into the debate surrounding Brian Mulroney's pitched battle to achieve a goal he'd set for himself early in his mandate as Prime Minister of Canada. He intended to right the great wrong done to the province of Québec when his rival Pierre Trudeau repatriated the Canadian constitution without Québec's signature. He wanted to heal the "humiliation of the Québécois" by giving that province special status in the Constitution.

Mulroney had failed to "bring Québec into Confederation" with the Meech Lake Accord. After almost eight years at the helm of a government battered by corruption, rampant patronage, and the dubious distinction of being the most despised government in Canadian history, Mulroney's only hope of pulling his career out of the political dumpster was to bring Québec into the constitutional bosom of the Canadian family. It would be his crowning glory. His entry into the history books as a great political leader. He was staking his future on the public's approval of the Charlottetown Accord in the October 26th referendum vote. Mulroney and Clark were dishing out promises of goodies to any and every group in exchange for a public declaration of support for the Yes side of the campaign.

But the Indians weren't playing ball. Status Indian leaders had their own agenda, and it was different from what the Métis leaders wanted. For years, the Métis leaders had been intensely jealous of all the rights enjoyed by status Indians. While the Métis National Council was using the Métis Accord to get what the Indians already had (a land base, attachment to the federal government instead of the provinces, and the right to self-government), the Indians were moving in another direction.

Even with the promise of entrenching a "general justifiable right to aboriginal self-government" thrown into the deal, the Assembly of First Nations was opposing the Accord. The self-government promise was vague. The terms were to be worked out at a later date, and self-government wasn't going to be legally enforceable for another ten years.

It wasn't that the national group representing Canadian Indians could really sway that many votes in support of the Accord. There are, after all, fewer than 400,000 treaty Indians in the entire country. What did count was the perception by the general public that the Accord was going to be a good deal for the First Nations people. Canadians had listened to too many horror stories of how Indian children had been beaten and sexually abused in residential schools, the Third World poverty on reserves, the uncomfortable acknowledgment that white governments had, for most of the 20th century, tried to deal with "the Indian problem" with policies that walked and talked a lot like cultural genocide. Canadians had been awash in white guilt for years. Good Canadians could be counted on to hold their noses over some of the more unpalatable parts of the Accord if they believed that the self-government package for Indians would right all the historical wrongs suffered by Canadian Indians in one fell swoop. All that uncomfortable guilt could be assuaged by simply ticking off the Yes box on the referendum ballot.

But First Nations leaders had good reason to be suspicious of what Mulroney was offering. They had too many questions that were going unanswered. They were being asked to trust in the honour and integrity of the Conservative government over issues like land claims and treaty rights. It was like the Indians were being asked to sign an irrevocable deal on a shiny new car without being allowed to get close enough to see if there was even an engine under the hood.

But all was not lost. Mulroney still had the Métis on side. After all, one aboriginal group is much like another in the public mind. The Métis could tap into liberal white guilt with their own story of cultural genocide masterminded by Sir John A. Macdonald, the persecution of their leader Louis Riel, who was hanged as a traitor when he was only trying to defend the rights of the Métis, and how the Métis had been robbed of their lands, humiliated by the white settlers.

For Mulroney, the Métis leaders were much easier to handle than the cranky and demanding Indian leaders. Yvon Dumont appeared more than willing to be cooperative.

Manitoba has always had a particularly strong position in the Métis political hierarchy, because the largest Métis population was historically centered in the Red River Settlement. Dumont held the reins of power not only of the Manitoba organization, but the Métis National Council as well. The presidents of the western Métis organizations got together in 1983 to create a national voice for the Métis, and a place alongside other national aboriginal groups like the Assembly of First Nations.

The MNC is the national arm of the Manitoba Métis Federation, the Pacific Métis Federation in British Columbia, the Métis Nation of Alberta, the Métis Society of Saskatchewan, and the Métis group from the Northwest Territories. (The Ontario Métis Aboriginal Association was a member, but folded after 1992.) The MNC is run by the five presidents, with the help of a couple of staff members.

As the MNC spokesperson, Dumont had a considerable amount of control over Métis politics in Western Canada. He had a vision of leading a great Métis nation…albeit an unrealistic one. Although groups like the Native Council of Canada also claimed to speak for all Métis in Canada, the MNC claimed all 300,000 Métis estimated to be living in the west. And it was Dumont who was invited to sit with the First Ministers during constitutional and aboriginal rights meetings, not the other Métis groups.

Individually, the Métis didn't have much political clout. Their numbers amounted to less than the population of a small city like Windsor. In truth, it didn't really matter to Mulroney how many Métis people Dumont was supposed to be speaking for, or even whether they could be counted on to vote for Charlottetown. What he needed was an aboriginal leader declaring support for the Accord. Mulroney knew he could count on Dumont. When the Prime Minister needed an aboriginal voice to support the Meech Lake Accord in 1989, Dumont had come through for him.

Meech Miracle

Most of Canada's Indians were vociferously opposed to Meech. They feared, with some justification, that if aboriginal rights were not entrenched in the constitution with Meech, it would never happen. Québec was going to get a constitutional veto over any future changes. Mulroney kept insisting Meech was the Québec round, and other issues would have to wait until the next round of the constitutional negotiations. But the unanimity clause (all ten fractious provinces had to agree on future changes), and the Québec veto virtually guaranteed that future changes to the constitution would be impossible.

Enter Dumont. Many Métis were just as strongly opposed to Meech as the Indians, but miraculously, Dumont was able to deliver unconditional Métis support for the Accord. When he appeared before the Manitoba Meech Lake Task Force in The Pas in 1989, Dumont's statement left no doubt that the MMF was 100 percent behind the Accord. For the Métis who thought they were rejecting Meech, Dumont's claim of support came as something of a surprise.

The Native Council of Canada roundly denounced Dumont's support of the accord. Council spokesperson Christopher McCormick said his organization represented 750,000 off-reserve Indians and Métis, and they were definitely not in favour of Meech. McCormick said Dumont had the right to his own personal opinion, but he needn't think his views were representative of those of the Métis.[1] MMF directors questioned Dumont's statement, too. At a board meeting in April, 1990, he was asked to explain where he'd gotten the mandate to support Meech. Dumont replied that it was discussed at the annual general assembly, and not questioned. Nor, said Dumont, had he heard any objections to Meech raised to various local and regional meetings he'd attended. The absence of objections from the membership he took as grounds for announcing they (and hence the MNC) were in favour of Meech.

The members weren't, of course. A furious Nelson Sanderson denounced Dumont in a letter mailed to all MMF members. The Métis activist said Dumont's "hasty decision" to throw Métis support behind Meech at the hearing in The Pas "reflects on a large number of Métis who stand in solidarity as aboriginal people and who feel they have not been adequately represented." But Dumont did not back down, or withdraw the Métis (or his) support of Meech.

Had Dumont sold out? There was little doubt in the minds of many Métis people that he had betrayed them by not representing their views. Regardless, Mulroney had what he needed—an aboriginal leader who supported his political objectives, and who could be counted on to appear when needed to provide aboriginal support.

Lesson Learned

Mulroney learned from his mistakes with Meech Lake. He wasn't going to be caught unprepared with Charlottetown. The federal government funded a huge pot of money for constitutional consultations. There would still be the same kind of parliamentary hearings held for Meech, but this time, lobby and advocacy groups were being given money to pay for their own consultations.

The Métis National Council was given a total of $5.8 million from the Secretary of State and the Special Joint Committee on a Renewed Canada to cover constitutional expenses for two years beginning April 1, 1991. Of that amount, $3.4 million was transferred to the provincial groups like the MMF for their constitutional costs, leaving the six MNC directors with $2.4 million for tthe national organization. That was on top of the MNC's regular funding from eight different government departments which totaled $1.2 million for the same two-year period. The "old boy's club," as one staff member called them, had copious quantities of cash to spend.

The MNC directors paid themselves very generous $300 per diems to attend meetings, an amount auditors later called excessive. Budget documents show the directors received total honoraria of $108,900 and, along with several staff members, spent just under $1 million on plane fares, cabs, limousines, dining, hotels, and meeting rooms. Another $687,000 was paid out in consulting fees.

Manitoba's share of the constitutional booty was used to fund public hearings. In the spring of 1991, four elders were appointed by the MMF as Métis senators. They had nothing to do with the Red Chamber, but were more like tribal elders. They were put in charge of organizing the hearings and preparing a report to go to the National Council. This time, Dumont was not going to be accused of not listening to the Métis people.

The Métis senate used the $653,000 funding from the MNC via the MMF to hold hearings and meet with people throughout Manitoba, and then produce a report. And the senators did a lot of travelling. They started official hearings in June, and by the end of July, they'd travelled 9,000 kilometres, attended 30 meetings and met with nearly a thousand people from 60 different organizations.[2] That resulted in considerable wear and tear on the "crusty old senators," as they referred to themselves.

By the time the senators had wrapped up Round Three, they'd done a very comprehensive job. As one staff person put it, it was the only real consultation the MMF ever did.

But the consultations were not about the broad-ranging implications of the Accord for Canada as a whole. The consultations were about Métis self-government and land rights. The extensive discussions with Manitoba Métis dealt with the Charlottetown Accord anywhere it affected Métis rights (or the rights Métis wanted). Métis support of the Accord seemed to be assumed. What the consultations produced was a massive support for Métis self-government and the acquisition of a land base as outlined in MNC's Métis Accord. The Charlottetown deal was there, in the back-ground, but it was being used as a vehicle for building a Métis empire on the Prairies under the control of the presidents of the provincial Métis organizations with, as always, Manitoba dominating.

And why wouldn't people support the Métis Accord? Certainly, they'd been primed to finally demand what they'd been told for years was their rightful due. Everyone was telling the Métis people that their time had come. Constitutional Affairs Minister Joe Clark who was also the minister responsible for the Métis, was going to speak for the the first time in St. Laurent in the summer of 1991. It was a cause for great excitement. The MMF regional office was hosting the event, and bought a piece of land on the edge of the village so it could set up a big meeting tent and have lots of room to put up campers and assemble a parade. But there was a glitch. There was no road access to the grounds.

At the same time, the MMF applied for a grant from the Manitoba Natural Resources department, headed by local MLA Harry Enns. It received the grant, $12,888, from a rare birds preservation fund. Natural Resources officials have refused to release details of the grant application, except to confirm it involved "heavy earth-moving equipment" to preserve a nesting area for the rare piping plovers in St. Laurent. However, municipal officials in St. Laurent say they have no record of any such presevation site and weren't aware of one. Natuaral Resources officials in St. Laurent admit they don't know where the site is either, and have never followed up on the grant application to find out how the money was spent.

Nevertheless, the road into the grounds for the annual assembly was completed just in time, and if there were any piping plovers nearby, they had to make way for the crowds gathered to hear Joe Clark's speech to the annual assembly.

"I am honoured as a Western Canadian to be with people who are in your phrase 'The Children of Canada,'" Clark told the MMF delegates, "but also people who have not been treated [well] in the past. I think representatives of both levels of government would admit this, and that justice is necessary."

Tom Berger fired up the masses at the same assembly with a report on his work on behalf of the land claim covering what used to be the Red River Settlement. Berger, a former Justice of the British Columbia Supreme Court who was a well-known advocate of native rights, started working on the land claim case in 1985. Referring to the land settlement deal in the Manitoba Act of 1870, Berger said the government deliberately stalled distributing the land to allow settlers from Ontario time to move in and take over. "They poured into Manitoba and gradually they became the majority," Berger told the Métis delegates.

> They took over the Manitoba legislature, and by this time seven years later, they said what the hell are we going to give 1.2 million acres to the Métis for. They are just a bunch of half breeds. To hell with them! We have gone through a lot of documents from the Chief Justice of Manitoba, and statements from very important figures in the Manitoba Government, saying that it was a big mistake ever to agree to let the Métis have any land. They do not know what to do with it anyway. They're just a bunch of no-goods... If Canada did not do the right thing a hundred years ago, it is not too late to do the right thing now, and to sit down with the Métis and negotiate a settlement of land claims.[3]

Later, in October, Mulroney arrived in Winnipeg for what Dumont characterized as the first time a Canadian prime minister had come to the Métis homeland to meet with Métis people. "...I wish I could reverse and rewrite a lot of chapters of Canadian history, 100, 150 and 200 years ago,"

Mulroney said. "But all we are given is the opportunity to try and write a little of our own. But in the process [we can] right some historic wrongs."[4]

A prime minister, a former prime minister and a former B.C. Supreme Court justice were promising to deliver power and money. Did the Métis people believe them?

While the Métis senate hearings in Manitoba heard mostly from people ardently supporting self-government (especially people who were directly involved in the MMF as employees or board members), there were also occasional voices expressing doubt. One man told the senate that he'd heard the promises of improved housing, better education, and more job opportunities over and over, and nothing ever happened. Why should he believe it was going to be any different this time? If there was any dissension in the ranks, they tended to be voices in the wilderness.

TURNING UP THE HEAT

By the summer of 1992, the Métis Accord had been finalized, complete with legal text and a detailed listing of the clauses in the Canadian constitution that would need to be amended to accommodate the Accord. But first, the Charlottetown deal had to win public approval in the October referendum. Dumont was doing his part. He appeared in Yes Campaign commercials that ran during *Hockey Night in Canada*. He campaigned in the trenches with Joe Clark.

Back home in Manitoba, the players in the MMF's inner political circle were abuzz with excitement. Word was spreading that a land claim settlement was on the table. Big money. Billions.

The MMF had first filed the land claim case in the courts in 1981, claiming rights to the lands of the old Red River Settlement. The lands, stretching from the American border to Lake Winnipeg, including the cities of Winnipeg and Portage la Prairie, were worth a lot of money. Some reports estimated $2 billion. Others were as high as $12 billion. But the whole case had been stalled for years. Suddenly, a settlement was supposed to be on the table without the claim even having to be proved in court.

Word was that Dumont had a special "in" with the Prime Minister. The MNC was working with Patrick MacAdam as its lobbyist, and MacAdam had been a close friend of Mulroney's since their college days at St. Francis

Xavier University in Nova Scotia. MacAdam was part of Mulroney's inner circle of friends, and that made him an influential lobbyist. If Dumont had the Prime Minister's ear, went the buzz, it was possible there really was a land deal was in the works. But it was all supposed to be hush-hush. No one was supposed to know about it.

Dumont nearly let the cat out of the bag himself at the annual assembly in St. Laurent in July of 1992 in his own excitement over the deal. He interrupted proceedings to read a letter he'd just received. It was from the Métis negotiating team. The Prime Minister was promising a deal. It is not clear if the delegates had any idea what deal he was referring to, but a close friend of Dumont told him as soon as he walked away from the microphone that he should never have read the letter out loud. Secrecy was crucial to the deal.

And what was the deal? According to insiders, the MNC was being given $15 million in September to quickly set up public hearings on a land claim settlement. Métis groups in other provinces had land claim ideas of their own, but the big claim was in Manitoba. The hearings were supposed to be completed by the end of December 1992, with the resultant report arriving at the conclusion that the predetermined amount of up to $10 billion was what the Métis people wanted. Based on the report, the Prime Minister was to announce a land claim settlement early in 1993.

The MMF land claim committee was in full panic. How the heck were they supposed to arrange the necessary hearings in such a short space of time? And how on earth were they supposed to spend $5 or $10 million dollars in just three months. The MMF's total annual operating budget wasn't even $5 million. And then there was the whole question of what to do with the $10 billion, and how to divide it up among the provinces.

According to a confidential document on the deal, the MNC was to establish an official position and alternatives for a settlement. That package would then be given "to the communities across the country, consulting with provincial organizations who will in turn consult with their members as to the tentative settlement package."[5]

In an August meeting, the land claims committee hashed out the MMF's role. The committee had to decide if it would allow the other provinces to piggyback their lesser claims on Manitoba's or insist that the MMF have its own deal. The consensus was that more money would come in a multi-provincial settlement, but they had to have an assurance that the MMF would get a minimum of $2 billion.

There were so many problems. Like all the people who would suddenly apply for membership in the Métis organizations with an eye on a share of the booty. Would there be land and money? Cash was better, but some small amount of symbolic land would be okay. And it was terribly important that everybody involved in the public hearings be singing out of the same song book. It had to be very clear who was in charge, and who would talk to the media. And what to do with the settlement money? The committee decided that it was a strong possibility "that the financial settlement if received would be put into a trust fund while using the substantial interest earned on the fund (for) education, economic development, land acquisition for the Métis people."[6]

The committee decided that as far as the consultation money was concerned

> ...the Land Claims Committee wants to ensure that the MMF receives at least one-third of the funds received by the MNC for the consultation process, given its efforts to establish a land claim and costs it incurred over the years for negotiations and initiation of its court action, efforts which brought us into the consultation process.[7]

But the provincial organizations weren't getting all the money. "It is acknowledged that advisor and consulting fees will take up at least five percent of the funds allotted, with the remainder to be divided among the provinces."[8] The documents do not say what the advisors and consultants would be doing in exchange for that three-quarters of a million dollars, nor were the recipients identified.

In a board meeting just prior to the assembly in St. Laurent in July of 1992, Dumont talked openly about his pending appointment as Manitoba's Lieutenant-Governor. George Johnson was approaching the end of his term in the vice-regal position, and was in poor health. Dumont was expecting the job. To take the position, Dumont would have to resign from both the MMF and MNC. It was, he told board members, "a difficult decision but...also a great honour for the Métis Nation."[9]

When Dumont addressed the MMF assembly the next day, he said, "I am pleased to report that we have had significant progress in our attempts to entrench self-government for Métis people in the Canadian constitution. We have met on a continuing basis throughout the spring of 1992 with the premiers and the Prime Minister, and with the Honourable Joe Clark, in an effort to ensure Métis participation. I can assure you that in the event the [Charlottetown] deal is reached, [it] includes the Métis."

But his same speech also contained a veiled warning to members in the audience who had other ideas about the future of the Métis. "To those others, who for their own practical purposes have decided to embark on a dangerous path, I challenge them to demonstrate their good faith.... I suggest further that the Métis Nation, in its wisdom, knows how to deal with such persons."

There was a serious fly in the ointment. L'Union Nationale Métisse Saint-Joseph du Manitoba, a group founded in 1887 to promote Métis culture and history, challenged the MMF's right to negotiate land claims and self-government for the Métis. In a letter sent out before the assembly to Mulroney, Clark, the provincial premiers and the leaders of aboriginal groups, L'Union president Augustine Abraham stated, "an inherent right to self-government, constitutionally included in conjunction with the proposed accord is, for the Métis, another word for segregation; indeed apartheid. It is completely contrary to the principles and vision of the founders of Manitoba."[10] She said it would simply impose dependency on the Métis. Louis Riel had negotiated provincial status for Manitoba and full citizenship for all the citizens.

"The Métis National Council or its member organizations," Abraham continued, "have no right to negotiate for themselves land claims which belong to all the descendants of the Red River Métis of 1870, since 90 percent of these people are not involved in any Métis organizations." As Louis Riel's grand-niece, Abraham was a force to be reckoned with. Or she would have been if Mulroney or Clark had been listening. No one was interested in the faint voices in the wilderness sounding discordant notes.

An empire was being created. Royalty wannabes were waiting anxiously in the wings to crown themselves as kings and queens of the new Métis nation with self-government and $10 billion in cash.

Real power. Real money. Real failure.

CHAPTER TWO

THE BUBBLE BURSTS

The Canadian public made its opinion of the Charlottetown Accord clear in the referendum vote. When the ballots were all counted, 54.4 percent of Canadians had given the thumbs-down to the deal. Even with the promise of the Métis Accord, the Métis showed no more inclination to support Charlottetown than the general population in western Canada. Even the folks in Yvon Dumont's home town of St. Laurent voted No.

Charlottetown was dead.

Constitutional Affairs minister Joe Clark had lots of explanations for the defeat of Charlottetown. He acknowledged the high level of public cynicism toward politicians in Canada as undermining the Yes side. He blamed misdirected anger over the Mulroney government's introduction of the despised Goods and Services Tax. He blamed former Prime Minister Pierre Trudeau who supported the No side. But, he said, the biggest problem with Charlottetown was its attempt to cover the interests of too many groups. Voters who had reservations about a certain issue, like senate reform or aboriginal self-government, rejected the whole package.[1]

But why would the Métis people reject Charlottetown? Perhaps because for Métis people not directly involved in the Manitoba Métis Federation, the promises of the Métis Accord had little meaning. The decades of messy political in-fighting within the organization had left many Métis with little expectation the organization would be able to deliver what it was promising. But Dumont wasn't about to roll over and play dead just because Charlottetown had gone down the tubes. He was doing his best to keep the vision of the Métis Nation alive. In the days following the referendum, Dumont pressured the federal and provincial governments to honour the unsigned Métis Accord. The Manitoba government refused to even consider the idea. The Métis Accord was, after all, part of the package that had been rejected in the referendum.

But Dumont insisted government support for self-rule was just as valid as before October 26. "They've all agreed that the Métis have been discriminated against…and we've been treated like second-class aboriginal people, and they've agreed that has to stop. It's still possible to bring this to an end."[2]

But no one was listening anymore. Exhausted from the Charlottetown effort, both politicians and the public had had a surfeit of constitutional talks, and the last thing anyone wanted to hear was any more debate involving the C-word.

Negotiations on self-government weren't completely over, however. Since 1987, the MMF had been receiving an annual grant of $630,000 from Ottawa and the Manitoba government for tripartite negotiations. That money hadn't been tied in any way to Charlottetown, and the cheques were still arriving at the MMF head office in Winnipeg. Self-government negotiations would simply continue on the same basis they had for the previous five years. And the land deal wasn't dead either. The promised money for consultations never arrived, but the deal was still being negotiated in the background, still very hush-hush.

The political future of the Mulroney government, and Mulroney himself, was in doubt. Fresh from a victory with Charlottetown and with constitutional amendments proceeding apace, Mulroney might have been able to swing the money promised in the land claims deal. So much would have been going on that $10 billion dollars might not have seemed too shocking an amount to suddenly shake loose from the federal treasury for the Métis. However, wounded and deflated in defeat, the likelihood of Mulroney making good on such a large deal was greatly diminished. But the deal was still on, and so was Dumont's pending appointment as Lieutenant-Governor. But Dumont was downplaying it. At an MMF board meeting two weeks after the referendum, he told directors it was "no more than at the stage of being a rumour."

Nonetheless, Dumont was carrying a cellular phone everywhere with him, just in case he got the PM's call. Dumont wasn't the only person in the running for the plum post. The seven Conservative MP's in Manitoba, party insiders and Premier Gary Filmon all had a say in making up the list on candidates, but the final decision was Mulroney's.

It wasn't a bad job either. The lieutenant-governor is the official head of state, representing Queen Elizabeth II, but the position holds little real political power. That remains in the hands of the premier and caucus. Nonetheless, it is one of the plum patronage appointments in Canada, considered second only to an appointment to the senate. Both are considered rewards to party loyalists, especially those whose political glory days are behind them. As Lieutenant-Governor, Dumont would be earning $83,000 a year for the five-year term, living expense-free in Government House next door to the Legislative Buildings, with aides, a chauffeur and car, and a budget for entertaining. Manitoba Conservatives and supporters like MP Jake Epp, Winnipeg Mayor Bill Norrie, and businessmen Kevin Kavanagh and Jack Fraser were all considered to be in the running.

Rumours of Dumont's impending appointment reached a full boil on November 16, the 107th anniversary of Louis Riel's hanging. Reporters covering the ceremony at Riel's grave in St. Boniface were expecting to go back to the newsroom with the story confirming a modern Métis leader was being honoured with the vice-regal position on the anniversary of the death of the Métis' most famous leader. Métis Senator Ferdinand Guiboche gave a stirring speech at Riel's graveside, telling the hundred people gathered there that Dumont's appointment "would be a very significant contribution. [It would reinforce] the feelings that we can belong, we can participate."[3] But there was no announcement, and no call from the Prime Minister.

For Dumont, the down side of taking the Vice-regal position was the requirement that he no longer be involved in anything political. As Lieutenant-Governor, he would have to give up his presidency of both the Manitoba Métis Federation and the Métis National Council, and resign from all the board positions he held on a variety of MMF-related corporations.

Close friends of the Dumont family say that wasn't a problem for Dumont. They say he was heartily sick of Métis politics, and he was worn out from the effort of juggling the Charlottetown deal, the Métis Accord, squabbling amongst the MNC provincial presidents, and fighting off directors with dollar signs in their eyes who wanted more power and more money for themselves.

Dumont may have been ready to take the new job, but friends say his wife Lyla was not. She apparently wanted him to push for a Senate appointment, a position where the family would not be uprooted and cast into a rigid, protocol-driven lifestyle so alien from the life they lived in St. Laurent. And a Senate appointment would provide long-term employment. As Lieutenant-Governor, Dumont would be heading back to his tire shop in St. Laurent after five years. But as a senator, 42-year-old Dumont would be able to put in 33 years holding down a chair in the Red Chamber.

Back at the head office, ambitious directors were jockeying to take over the presidency and control of the organization. Because a regular election was scheduled for 1993, the board would elect an interim president from amongst themselves to head the MMF until the election. For the insiders, it was important that one of their own, someone who knew how the game was played, take over as president.

Interlake vice-president Robert Gaudry was the chosen one. That's what he told directors as he lobbied for their support. Some of the directors were not too impressed. They considered the less-than-articulate Gaudry a poor public spokesperson for the MMF. They wanted someone with more polish, someone like director Ernie Blais. In the background was Billyjo Delaronde, the man who'd served as Dumont's principal secretary and assistant for many years—the man credited with delivering Dumont's support at election time. And Delaronde was hurting. He told a number of people that his old friend Yvon was leaving him behind, that Yvon was being rewarded with a job as Lieutenant-Governor and he was getting nothing.

Dumont's appointment as Lieutenant-Governor was confirmed by the Prime Minister on January 22, 1993. The *Winnipeg Free Press* pronounced it "a good appointment," and waxed poetic in an uncharacteristically misty-eyed editorial:

> Louis Riel sent his troops to stop lieutenant governor William McDougall at Pembina in 1869 because Riel and his people did not accept the constitutional program of John A. Macdonald's government, which McDougall had come to enforce. Yvon Dumont in 1989 accepted the constitutional program of Brian Mulroney's government in the Meech Lake Accord and the Charlottetown Accord because that program included self-government for aboriginal people including the Métis. As a result, Mr. Dumont has been appointed as Mr. McDougall's remote successor.[4]

The timing was right for an aboriginal leader to take the position. To the general public, Dumont's appointment was viewed as heart-warming gesture to the Métis who had been so badly treated in the creation of Canada.

But the MMF had business to attend to. The entire 23-member board and senior staff flew out to Vancouver for the transfer-of-power board meeting, along with senior staff members. When the meeting was over, Gaudry was supposed to be the new president. However, that's not what happened. When the election process started, Gaudry was nominated. So was Blais. And then South-East region vice-president Denise Thomas. Delaronde couldn't run for office himself because he was staff, nor could he nominate candidates. He encouraged another director to nominate Thomas.

The first vote was a tie. Each nominee received seven votes, but the constitution dictated the interim president had to receive at least fifty percent of the vote. A second ballot was called, with the person receiving the fewest votes being dropped. This time, the vote was 8, 7, 6...Blais, Gaudry, Thomas. In the third ballot, Blais won by an unknown margin. The ballots were destroyed.

He wasn't supposed to win. He wasn't an insider. He wasn't one of the inner circle. Several directors said later that Blais had won support amongst the larger number of non-insiders because they were fed up with the way the insiders had been running the MMF. There had been too many shady deals, too many secret deals the board was told about only after the fact, too many stories of internal corruption and fraud, too many distasteful examples of the lengths board members would go to keep hold of their positions. Blais was promising to clean up the MMF and get it back on track, and there were enough directors prepared to give him a chance.

Blais' election was a shock to the insiders, but there wasn't much they could do about it until the general election. They were nervous, though, because Blais suddenly had access to a lot of information that could be damaging to some directors' political careers—and it could be used against them in the election.

And suddenly, the $10 billion land claim deal disappeared. Poof! Gone. How could the insiders be trusted to handle such a large amount of money if they couldn't even handle something as simple as Gaudry's pre-arranged election?

But all was not lost. All they had to do was stonewall the new president until the fall. They could make it very difficult for him to find out anything they didn't want him to know about, like the operations of some of the

MMF's corporations. Blais said later he was refused access to financial records to important companies like the Manitoba Métis Community Investments Inc., a subsidiary of the MMF set up in 1984 to handle commercial and industrial investments.

When election time rolled around in October, the inner circle fully expected to have their own president, Billyjo Delaronde, in place. It was a bitter and divisive battle in the Métis community—a battle between the old order that wanted full control back and those Métis who were promising to "clean up" the MMF and saw the election as a real opportunity for change.

After the ballots were counted, Blais was once again president, but the elected board was split right down the middle between his supporters and those of the old power block. The board was hamstrung. It was impossible to accomplish any business. But the insiders weren't beaten. Not by any stretch. At the annual assembly on November 12, they put forward a board motion to oust Blais as president. It passed, 13-9.

Blais' rivals had changed the locks on the offices earlier that day, expecting Blais to accept the board vote, but he refused to resign. The annual assembly descended into total chaos as the factions screamed at each other across the conference room.

Blais finally agreed to step down, but only if the entire board of directors resigned as well. On December 8 in The Pas, the board voted unanimously to resign and await a new election.

It appears the directors thought they would continue running their regional offices and keep their jobs, even though the board had disbanded. But the courts thought otherwise. On December 23, the Court of Queen's Bench ruled the MMF was unable to conduct its own affairs because without a board of directors, there was no one with the legal capacity to conduct any business. The judge stated clearly that when the directors had resigned from the MMF board, they'd also resigned from their positions as directors of the regional corporations. The regional vice-presidents and directors didn't have the legal authority to take ten dollars out of petty cash, never mind run their offices.

The MMF was without a leader, and business operations had come to a skidding halt. The wheels had fallen off the cart. In the space of one short year, the MMF had gone from leading the Métis movement in both land claims progress and self-government to being completely impotent. The courts had to appoint an interim board because the Métis couldn't run their own organization. The vision of a great Métis nation shattered.

What happened? For those who had participated in MMF politics, those who'd been part of the game, those who'd come to view the whole organization with fear and distaste, the collapse of the MMF had been a long time coming. But it had been inevitable.

To understand the whole story, perhaps the best place to start is at the beginning. And that goes back more than three centuries.

Chapter Three

In the Beginning

It was a race whose length of history matched that of the white man on this continent. Scholars searching for the roots of the hybrid race heard again and again that the Métis nation, if such it could be called, was born exactly nine months after the first white man arrived.[1]

There are those who believe the psyche of the modern Métis still carries the stigma of illegitimate birth. The bastard race. Second class.

The arrival of the white man in north-western Canada began in 1670 when King Charles II granted a vast tract of land called Rupert's Land to the Hudson's Bay Company. Scottish fur traders working for Hudson's Bay and French fur traders from the rival North West Company formed alliances with Ojibway and Cree women, and their children became the first Métis, or mixed blood.

There were some native marriages, but in the wilds of the North-West, there were no clergymen to conduct traditional marriages. Neither were there court officials who could conduct civil services. In the absence of church law, matrimony did not wait for ritual or ceremony. Consenting parties married "according to the custom of the country" by simply moving in together to occupy the same tent or teepee, and dissolving the alliance required little more than moving out.[2] It was an arrangement that suited the men who had come to a strange and wild land where no white women lived. But there was a commercial as well as personal benefit to the pairing up of Indian women and white men. Many fur traders found it convenient to take a wife who was the daughter of the chief or tribal leader. Because of the loyalties of the clan system, traders found Indians more amenable to trading with people who'd married into their families.

In truth, women were crucial to the survival of traders. Services could not be bought from tradespeople or shops. There weren't any. Indian women had the task of preserving the meat and fish brought home by hunters, gathering roots and berries, caring for small gardens, tanning hides, making clothes, bearing children and raising them.[3] Before long, small communities of Halfbreed families sprang up around the forts that dotted the northwest, relying on the trading posts for employment and what little medical care was available. Métis children had the enviable status of being bicultural. They had feet in both the Indian and European cultures.

> The more intelligent boys learned to read and write and were sought after as clerks by the local trading company. The others, through their fathers' connections, would have the preferred jobs such as interpreters, canoesmen, fur packers and manual workmen around the fort. Those who could not secure such positions were able to enter trapping on a competitive basis with their Indian relatives. Such Métis became indispensable to the Indians, for through them the Indians could negotiate more effectively with local traders. Through them they had access to some of the technological knowledge of the White man. Indeed many of the early Métis were chosen as chiefs of tribes because of their knowledge and understanding of White culture so urgently needed by the Indians.[4]

Some of the servants (or employees) of the Hudson's Bay and North West companies sent their eldest sons home to England, Scotland, France, or east to Canada to be educated. Many, as outlined in the following letter written by a priest with the Anglican Missionary at Lower Church in the Red River Settlement, took less care of the progeny they fathered. The letter was sent to the Church Missionary Society in 1833. Reverend W. Cockran noted that in the summer, the traders were kept busy transporting furs they had acquired from the Indians to the trading posts and forts.

> During the summer there was plenty of opportunities for the young voyageur to give vent to his licentious passions; at every post he

will find women who will do anything for hire. He had no principles to contend with; he therefore finds it easy to do what is most pleasant to corrupt nature and most popular with his companions.

When the young voyageur comes to his winter quarters, he finds he wants many things to fit him for this new existence which he had entered upon. He wants his leather coat, trowsers, mittens, duffle socks and shoes, all then must be made and kept in repair. He has no time to do this himself; he applies to an Indian who had got some daughters, or two or three wives; here he is quick served, he makes a present to the head of the family, they set to work, and make all ready for him, he comes a certain time for his clothes, brings a little rum, and makes the principal persons of the family merry.

He sleeps there, and out of gratitude and courtesy, the old woman puts her daughter to bed to him, or the Indian may give him one of his three wives, who lays under his displeasure; thus the unfortunate voyageur forms his connexion with the natives, and raises the offspring. He may continue there for two or three years, and enjoy the benefit of his helpmate. He goes off in the summer, returns in the autumn, and perhaps finds the same young woman given to another. This does not distract his mind, he forms another connexion as speedily as possible; by this time he believes that he cannot get on without a woman.

The next time he leaves for his winter quarters, he perhaps is sent to a post 600 or 1000 miles from all his former wives; he forgets them at once, and serves himself for the time being, with the first that comes to hand—he looks for neither beauty or virtue; if she is woman, that is sufficient.

The same course is run until old age and grey hairs are upon him; his body emaciated with the fatigues of voyaging, and means too scanty to cast a robe once a year over all his adulterous progeny. His case being desperate, he thinks of making an effort to remedy the errors of 30 or 40 years, by one mighty struggle. Out of his many connexions he finds some one that ranks above the rest. He selects her to be the companion of his old age; collects his multifarious progeny from the ends of the earth, (for he has been every where through all this Continent) and bends his course to Red River, with worn out constitution, with small means, with a woman that knows none of the duties of civilized life, with a dispirited family who know nothing but what the heathen have taught them, who have no interest in each other's welfare, to begin life anew, to learn with his heathen family how to discharge his duty to God, his neighbour, and his own soul.[5]

The offspring of an Indian woman and a man from Scotland, Ireland, or England, was generally referred to as a Halfbreed, the children of an Indian and French liaison, Métis. And the birth of this new race proceeded apace.

...the women of all tribes did not regard motherhood as a great burden and had no objections to big families. The rate at which the Métis and Halfbreed populations grew was proof enough. Just 132 years after La Verendrye paddled up the Red River to build Fort Rouge where Winnipeg now stands, the small and new province of Manitoba was shown by census to have more people of the mixed race than of all others combined..many more.[6]

Many homespun marriages were simple matters of convenience, and men had little compunction about leaving whenever it suited them. And the validity of those unhallowed marriages between a white man and an Indian woman were long in doubt. The abandoned and abused wife had no recourse in law.[7] The children of these alliances were neither European nor Indian, but had the unique characteristics described in 1856 by Alexander Ross, a prominent member of the Red River colony:

They cordially detest all the laws and restraints of civilized life, believing all men were born to be free In their own estimation, rather are all great men, and wonderfully wise: and so long as they wander about on these wild and lawless expeditions [buffalo hunts], they will never become a thoroughly civilized people, nor orderly subjects in a civilized community. Feeling their own strength from being constantly armed, and free from control, they despise all others; but above all, they are marvelously tenacious of their own original habits. They cherish freedom as they cherish life.[8]

The Red River Settlement along the Red and Assiniboine Rivers became a centre for trade and commerce. In 1811, HBC sold a large chunk of Rupert's Land, including the Red River valley, to the Earl of Selkirk. Selkirk wanted to establish a farming settlement along the Red. The arrival of the first wave of settlers in 1812 and 1813 was a taste of things to come for the Métis.

It was efforts by settlers to restrict Métis hunting and trading practices (along with some agitation stirred up by the North West company to upset business with the rival HBC) that eventually led to the Métis taking up arms against the settlers. The battle of Seven Oaks in 1816 could be viewed as either a victory by Cuthbert Grant and his Métis followers, or the massacre of 20 settlers and the area governor. But the purpose was served. The settlers who survived immediately left.

Selkirk returned with a small army of hired soldiers. To solidify his place in the valley, Selkirk signed a land surrender treaty in 1817 with the local Cree and Saulteaux chiefs. In exchange for one hundred pounds of tobacco paid annually to each tribe, the Indians ceded two miles on both sides of the Red River from Grand Forks to Lake Winnipeg, and two miles on both sides of the Assiniboine River from the junction at the Red west to Rat River (near present-day Portage la Prairie).[9] The Hudson's Bay Company honoured the Selkirk Treaty, delivering the annual tobacco allotments, and granting parcels of land within the settlement boundaries.

In 1821, the Hudson's Bay and North West companies amalgamated, and the end of competition meant the closure of many of the forts and trading posts. The majority of the mixed race families packed up and made the long trip to the Red River Settlement. They came from all corners of the northwest—from what is now known as the North West Territories, Alberta, Saskatchewan, Montana and the Dakotas.

Although the settlement was split along ethnic and religious lines—the Catholic Métis and the Protestant Halfbreeds—the need to form an alliance against the all-powerful Hudson's Bay Company and the increasing number of immigrant settlers arriving in the area was greater than their differences. Both represented a threat to their freedom to trade with whomever they pleased, and their right to roam the prairies at will.

There was no elected government in the territory. It was under the governance of the Hudson's Bay Company. The only form of government recognized by the Métis was the system used to organize buffalo hunts. The hunts were crucial to Métis survival, for food and hides for their own use.

The buffalo also provided highly-valued pemmican and hides for trade. The annual hunts were tightly organized, with a clear chain of command. Because the hunts sometimes lasted for a month and involved 300 or 400 men, women and children, it was important that the whole unit be contained and controlled. But beyond the hunt, any kind of formalized government was not considered. Rather, many Métis followed the Indian way of community, traveling in family groups, so that like the Cree or Ojibway, there would be the Ducharme tribe or the McKay tribe.

The Métis were traders who brought their business to the Red River Settlement, or transported goods to and from St. Paul in Minnesota. The Red River carts used on the buffalo hunts became the chief form of freight transport, with "trains" of up to 300 squeaky-wheeled carts. The carts went south loaded with furs, pemmican, dried buffalo meat, moccasins and garments decorated with beadwork, and returned with groceries, tobacco, liquor, dry goods, ammunition, farm implements and such luxuries as window glass and pianos.[10]

But it was a way of life coming to an end. The Canadian government's plan was to colonize the West and establish agriculture-based communities. As more and more people arrived to break sod and set up homesteading, the buffalo herds moved farther west. And in the federal government's thinking, according to Métis historians like Bruce Sealey and Doug Sprague, the nomadic Métis people simply did not fit into the settlement plans for the West. Settlers were moving in to take over lands Métis families had simply assumed was theirs, although they held no title or legal right to the property by any formal land grants or purchases.

The right to land and the right to freely hunt and trade were key demands of the provisional government formed by Louis Riel during the brief period in 1869 when the Hudson's Bay Company had withdrawn, but before the Government of Canada took control of the territory. The provisional government, says MMF education coordinator Audreen Hourie, was quickly established by following the familiar system used during the buffalo hunt. Louis Riel has become a romantic figure in Manitoba's history…a great political leader, a Father of Confederation, a traitor, a madman. His story has captured the imaginations of many writers and is well-documented elsewhere. But what he tried to do was ensure the Métis of the Red River Settlement were given some protection from the expected influx of European settlers.

By 1870, there were almost 12,000 people in the postage stamp-sized province: 5,757 Métis, 4,083 Halfbreeds, 1,565 whites and 558 Indians. The mixed races accounted for 82 percent of the population. Riel wanted a guarantee that the people in the Red River Settlement would be given recognized land rights that wouldn't be swept away in the onslaught of settlers eager to stake land for themselves. That right was enshrined in the Canadian constitution as the Manitoba Act of 1870. Métis historians like Sealey and Sprague say that despite promises from the Prime Minister, Sir John A. Macdonald, few Métis ended up with much of anything.

Thomas Berger, who has been hired to handle the Manitoba Métis Federation's land claim court case based on what was promised in the Manitoba Act, describes events this way:

> Now, there was an uprising at Red River where the Métis, led by Louis Riel, formed a provisional government. Delegates of the provisional government went to Ottawa, to negotiate with John A. Macdonald, the first prime minister of Canada, and George Etienne-Cartier, and they worked out a deal. And the deal was designed to protect everybody here at Red River in what was later to be Manitoba.
>
> There were to be two official languages, English and French. The schools of the Protestants and the Catholics were to be maintained out of public funds. And the Métis, who knew there was going to be a wave of white settlement coming into the Northwest, into the Red River, once Canada acquired this vast area, wanted guarantees for their land, the land they held, the river lots, and for the future generations of Métis that would come along.
>
> Now, all that was in the deal. What happened was that the Parliament of Canada passed an act called the Manitoba Act which incorporated all these arrangements. The Manitoba Act, since 1870, has been as much a part of the constitution of Canada as the Charter of Rights is today.[11]

In fact, it was only in 1985 that the Supreme Court ruled that Manitoba did indeed have to honour the Manitoba Act by providing services in two official languages, and not until 1994 did francophones have a separate school board.

The Manitoba Act outlined the land in the Red River Settlement that was to be given to the Métis, and was defended by the Prime Minister in the

Parliamentary debate on the Manitoba Act:

> There shall…out of the lands there, be a reservation for the purpose of extinguishing the Indian title, of 1,400,000 acres. That land is to be appropriated as a reservation for the purpose of settlement by half-breeds and their children of whatever origin….
>
> This Bill contains very few provisions, but not too few for the object to be gained, which is the quiet and peaceable acceptance of a new state of things by the mass of people there and the speedy settlement of the country by hardy emigrants from all parts of the civilized world.[12]

It's not clear that Riel ever considered the land settlement as an extinguishment of aboriginal title. That idea appears to have originated with Abbé N.J. Ritchot who, along with John Black and Alfred Scott, were delegated by the provisional government to negotiate the terms of the Manitoba Act. Ritchot admitted in his speech to the Legislative Assembly of Assiniboia in June of 1870 that he wasn't sure about the Métis having an aboriginal entitlement, but he felt it was the best way to get it through the House of Commons.[13]

The Métis in the Red River Settlement were the children of marriages between Europeans and Indians from all across the north-west, as well as Indians from Manitoba. Government officials questioned how the Manitoba Act could extinguish an aboriginal entitlement based on Indian ancestry from another part of the country. There was a basic question about whether the land settlement being given to the Métis had anything to do with aboriginal ancestry at all, or whether it was an acknowledgment of the contribution of early settlers to the area. By referring to the land grant in the Manitoba Act as "a reservation for the purpose of extinguishing the Indian Title" in parliament, the Prime Minister reinforced the perception that the Métis were being given land based on their Indian ancestry, and the idea they were being given a large single block of land like an Indian reserve.

In parliament, the opposition challenged the notion that Métis people had inherited Indian title and pointed out that a huge Métis land reserve in Manitoba, along with the Indian reserves, the land reserves for HBC and confirmation of title for settlers already there would effectively landlock any further settlement opportunities.[14] Rather than create a Métis enclave in Manitoba, the Manitoba Act conferred 1.4 million acres upon "the children of half-breed heads of families" in 240-acre parcels without any restriction on the sale of the parcels other than the general property law of Manitoba.[15]

Those who argue the Métis were cheated of their lands say the federal government should not have permitted the Métis to sell the land, so it would be protected for future generations of Métis. It appears quite clear, however, that what Riel sought was to prevent the Métis from coming under the paternalistic control of the federal government. He did not want the Métis to be bundled off to reserves like the Indians.

Thomas Flanagan, who has written extensively on Native politics and history, notes the latter-day issue of acquiring aboriginal rights for the Métis often obscures the status the Métis did have. "When Manitoba entered Confederation, the Métis were British subjects with full civil and political rights, and all the attendant responsibilities. Unlike Indians, they could own land in severalty, enter into contracts, vote and hold public office."[16]

Flanagan was hired by the federal Department of Justice in 1986 as a consultant on the land claims case brought by the Manitoba Métis Federation. Flanagan was concerned his work for one side of the land claims issue might bring the accuracy of his research into question; however, he noted that all the published research on which the MMF was basing its case had been produced by employees of the MMF, by scholars under contract, or by people sympathetic to the Métis movement. Still, he noted, in the end the research has to be able to stand on its own, regardless for the motives of undertaking it.

Nonetheless, Flanagan's conclusions about Métis land issues tended to be quite different from those of writers like Bruce Sealey. (Sealey's books were published by the Manitoba Métis Federation Press, later renamed Pemmican Publications. Both Sealey and Doug Sprague are long-time directors of the publishing company.)

The government's attempts to divide up and distribute land following proclamation of the Manitoba Act in 1870 met with all kinds of complications. In trying to right a wrong, government officials would often only make matters worse.

At the same time as officials were trying to figure out how to distribute the land, immigrants were streaming into the settlement, often not clear on where they could or could not claim land. The original settlers who weren't included in the Métis land grant complained, and were added. Since it seemed unfair to exclude the Métis family heads from receiving some benefit, the government added cash scrip at a value of $160 each for the Métis and the original white settlers. The land went to the children. Sprague and Sealey both say the Métis were swindled of their land and their scrip stolen. Flanagan argues that indeed some degree of thievery and fraud did take place, but he notes it was often the land speculators cheating each other. Flanagan also argues that the sale of Métis lands has to be viewed in the light of a massive influx of settlers and the resultant land boom. It took the government years to investigate and settle land patents on Métis children, and in the meantime, some sold their children's land. Some children came of age and sold land that had doubled in value to land speculators.

Flanagan says many Métis did very well by the land settlement. He cites the example of Cyril Marchand, his wife and nine children, who had claims to three river lots in St. Norbert. Both parents were entitled to $160 dollars of cash scrip. Each of the children was entitled to 240 acres of land, and Marchand's three lots amounted to 594 acres. He also received scrip in lieu of hay rights totaling $387. The benefits to the Marchand family totaled 2,754 acres of land and $707 in scrip. This was at a time when an average worker with a steady job was earning about $500 a year, and an average settler was working an 80-acre farm.

Many Métis left the Red River Settlement, following their traditional lifestyle farther west. But did they leave because they didn't care for the restrictions of farm and urban life, or were they driven out by settlers and land speculators? As of the writing of this book, the land claims case has yet to be heard by the courts.

The Métis National Council calls the exodus the first Métis diaspora. The word diaspora is defined as "Jewish people who live outside the Holy Land." It's not clear if the MNC is comparing the movement of Métis out of Red River to the exile of Jews from the Holy Land, or whether the MNC considers any Métis not living in the Red River settlement as driven from the Métis Homeland. The Métis who left Red River scattered widely, some going to Minnesota and the Dakotas, more moving to what would later become Saskatchewan and Alberta.

The second Métis diaspora, says the MNC, followed the failed Northwest rebellion in 1885 led by Louis Riel. Again the pressure of homesteading settlers pushed the Métis still pursuing the traditional nomadic lifestyle farther west, north and south.

The Prime Minister was not in the mood to deal with the Métis as a political entity then. Macdonald no longer needed to quickly negotiate an agreement as he had in 1869. The surge of settlers had long since passed through the Red River Settlement, and the Métis at Batoche presented no barrier to further colonization. Impatiently, Macdonald declared the Métis nonexistent. "If they are Indians, they go with the tribe," he told the House of Commons in 1885. "If they are half-breeds, they are whites, and they stand in exactly the same relation to the Hudson's Bay Company and Canada as if they were altogether white."[17]

Homesteaders were taken up with settling in their newly-adopted land, and were generally unaware of the history and culture of the people who had lived on the land before them. The Métis who had settled well—those who had taken up farming in the fertile lands of the Red River Valley, those who had become part of the middle class as merchants or shopkeepers—were assimilated into the burgeoning community of Winnipeg.

There are tales of Métis who were harassed in the streets by white immigrants for being Indians, Halfbreeds or, if associated with Riel, traitors. Hourie, MMF's researcher and education coordinator, says the soldiers sent to Red River in 1870 by Macdonald hunted down and persecuted Métis people. She says the presence of the military and fear of persecution forced Métis people to obscure their Métis-ness and speak the languages of Michif French only in their homes. Hourie says Michif French (French blended with Cree) was kept alive in St. Boniface by the Métis who identified themselves publicly as French-Canadian. In fact, says Hourie, many of the people in St. Boniface today can trace their roots to the Métis of the Red River.

She's right. An organizer with western Canada's biggest winter fêtes, the Festival du Voyageur, says one of the biggest selling points to international markets is the fact that most of the people involved in the Festival are seventh-generation descendants of the original voyageurs. But that festival is publicly perceived as French-Canadian, not Métis.

ROAD ALLOWANCE PEOPLE

The most visible Métis in the late 1800s and the early years of the 1900s were the poor, the uneducated and the landless. By European standards, the Métis were "idle, dissipated, unreliable and ungrateful...possessing extraordinary powers of endurance…yet scarcely to be depended on in critical moments, superstitious and ignorant."[18] The nomadic people were relegated to unclaimed land on the fringes of civilization or along road allowances. The rest of the land had been claimed. Shantytowns made up of makeshift houses built with whatever was at hand sprang up on the edges of the larger towns. If all most of the public saw of the Métis were the down-and-outers, it's probably not surprising that the terms Métis and Halfbreed moved from simply being descriptive to being derogatory.

During the Depression, the abject poverty of the Métis was seen as a national disgrace. They were the poorest of the poor. The Alberta Royal Commission looked at ways to help the Métis, but the commissioner made it clear that the Métis he was concerned about were those "having Indian Blood in their veins and living the normal life of a half-breed…You see, you must include living the life of a half-breed, otherwise…there are a large number of men in Edmonton, some occupying responsible positions, who are not intended to be included in this investigation."[19]

Eventually, Canadians simply forgot about the other Métis. The ones who weren't poor and destitute, living on the edges of Indian reserves, or squatting in hovels on Crown land. People like Premier John Norquay and Captain William Kennedy made their marks on Canadian history; however, they are rarely acknowledged as famous Métis. But the Métis left an indelible mark on prairie history. In fact, Bruce Sealey says they were the first Natives of Canada, not the Indians. He says the Indians and Europeans were both just immigrants, albeit a millennium apart.[20]

As the 19th century progressed, Métis had long since ceased to be a political force of any kind in Canada and, in 1941, the Dominion Bureau of Statistics dropped the term Métis from its census forms. The Métis had become the forgotten people.

CHAPTER FOUR

THE MÉTIS, REDISCOVERED

The "rediscovery" of aboriginal people in Canada can be traced directly to the civil rights movement in United States. The battle by Black Americans for the right to vote, the right to sit in any restaurant they wanted, to hold any job regardless of their race raged across the continent. In the mid-1960s, Canadians were treated to nightly television newscasts of race riots in cities like Chicago and Detroit and the Watts ghetto of Los Angeles; the memorable and poignant picture of a little black girl in a lacy white dress, with school books in hand, being escorted by the National Guard into what was no longer going to be an all-white school; the words of Martin Luther King Jr. at a freedom rally in Washington, "I have a dream...."

In the U.S., Black Americans were in a full scale battle with government and the white majority over racial discrimination. Canadians sympathized with the Black movement, and they could hardly ignore the discrimination against minorities in their own country. The most visible and vocal were the Indians. Canadians could hardly denounce Americans for not allowing Blacks the right to vote. Indians in Canada had just acquired the right to vote in federal elections in 1960.

The aboriginal advocacy groups that formed in in the late 1950s and early 1960s generally included status Indians, non-status Indians, Métis and Inuit, even though each group had a different agenda. Status Indian leaders wanted control over their reserves and the money to run them, recognition of treaty rights and land claims, and the right to vote. The Métis, on the other hand, had acquired full British citizenship when Manitoba became a province, with all the rights enjoyed by every other Canadian.

They had the right to vote. What the Métis leaders wanted was recognition as aboriginals and access to some of the benefits the Indians were getting from the federal government. The Indian leaders wanted to be treated more like white people. The Métis leaders wanted to be treated more like Indians.

Caught between Indians and Métis were non-status Indians, people who for whatever reason had lost their treaty rights, or never received them. They, too, had a different agenda. At the time, an Indian woman who married a white man or a non-status Indian immediately lost her status. Similarly, if an Indian woman bore a child the band council believed to be fathered by someone other than a treaty Indian, that child had no status. Some were disenfranchised because they or their fathers had sold their status rights back to the government, or they'd been forced to give up status to join the military. Non-status Indians were focused on regaining or acquiring status they felt they deserved. The status Indians and the Métis found it particularly difficult to work together in a single organization because their goals were so different. That, in the end, is what gave rise to the Manitoba Métis Federation.

The government money and the need to serve the specific needs of the Métis came together during an Indian and Métis conference in Winnipeg at the Marlborough Hotel in 1967. The annual meetings of natives had started in 1954, but the conflicting agendas of the Indians and Métis had become too much for Métis rancher Angus Spence.

Furious that the whole conference was focused on the Indians, Spence is said to have walked up to the front of the room and announced, "There's nothing here for us. All we're doing is talking about the Indian Act. I'm going across the hallway, and I'm asking anyone who wishes to join me."[1] Spence walked out of the meeting, followed by about 20 people. They were setting up their own organization specifically for the Métis. Or at least that's one version of events. Another version has the Indians throwing the Métis out because they wanted an organization solely for status Indians, and the Métis and non-status Indians were getting in the way.

In 1967, Jean Chretien, the Indian Affairs minister in the Trudeau government, was laying the groundwork for the release of a White Paper in 1969 proposing assimilation as the best way to deal with the "Indian problem." The federal government knew it was going to run into a lot of flak from Indians with that idea, and decided it needed friendly Indian organizations to help ease public acceptance of the idea. In *Paper Tomahawks*, a controversial book detailing the creation of the Manitoba Indian Brotherhood, author Jim Burke suggests that Indian organizations were being set up in the 1960s solely to create an Indian voice that the government could control for its own benefit.

> Reserves were to be abolished and the Department of Indian Affairs phased out through a bilateral agreement of the two "partners" who would chart the future course for Canada's Indians. And who were these partners? The Department of Indian Affairs and the Indian associations of Canada which would, theoretically, serve as the collective voice of the country's registered Indians. But first, Indian organizations had to be restructured into vehicles which would advance Ottawa's assimilation designs.... In the fall of 1967, the machinery was set in motion to establish an organization of registered Indians in [Manitoba]....[2]

Once the Métis left the Winnipeg meeting, willingly or otherwise, the Indians promptly resurrected the defunct Manitoba Indian Brotherhood and elected a new executive. They were ready to play ball. The bait? Money. Lots of it.

In 1969, MIB was getting $125,000 from Indian Affairs, but by the end of 1972, combined government grants gave the organization an annual budget of over one million dollars. MIB had assumed the right to speak for all status Indians in Manitoba. After all, it had the government's ear and the government's money. The set-up worked well for the Indian Affairs minister and his bureaucrats. If they needed to assure the general public that Indians were on-side with the issue of the day, all they had to do was trot out the leaders of the Indian organizations the government had set up. And if Indian Affairs needed to bring doubting and suspicious band chiefs on-side, they had Indian leaders in place to persuade the chiefs that organizations like MIB were working hard to defend their interests.

For many Indians, organizations like the MIB had become nothing more than an extension of the federal government, a "brown bureaucracy." The leaders were labeled "Uncle Tomahawks" by Indian activists who figured they'd sold out to government interests.

In the mid-1960s, the Métis didn't count for much on the national political scene. Métis "empowerment" was more of a provincial issue. Well before the move toward re-establishing a Métis identity resulted in the forming of an organization in Manitoba, the provincial government had been looking for a way to deliver economic development programs to disadvantaged parts of the province. Governments had lots of money in those days, and were looking for ways to spend it.

In the 1950s, Manitoba created Community Development Programs to help communities through planned stages of development. The idea was to help people in a particular community identify what they needed to improve their lot, then a Community Development Worker would help them figure out what they could manage with their own resources and where to look for outside help. The worker would also help people to understand the complexities of dealing with government bureaucracies.[3] The program met with little tangible success.

In 1959, the Manitoba Department of Agriculture and Immigration commissioned a study to identify aboriginal people in the province, the better to target government aid. The study, written by John Legasse, made it very clear that in identifying Métis people, consideration was only being given to those who met the criteria established by earlier government commissions: people of mixed white and aboriginal ancestry, living much like Indians. In other words, only the poor and marginalized. Legasse noted that by his estimation, that described only about 20 percent of the Métis in Manitoba. So who were the other 80 percent? They were the successful Métis—the doctors, government bureaucrats, librarians, shopkeepers and housewives, largely urban people who were doing reasonably well on their own, without government assistance.

The government was only interested in poor Métis, the ones living in shanties on the edges of reserves, or in small remote communities where they eked out a living trapping, fishing or selling wood. They were interested only in the Métis who were illiterate and living in poverty. According to one Métis old-timer, it was the provincial government that first sought to set up the Manitoba Métis Federation. It was to be an organization used to deliver government programs to the disadvantaged Métis identified in Legasse's study. The government could then show Oppositions critics and the public what they were doing for the poor Métis.

Métis Jean Allard was elected as MLA for Rupertsland in 1969 when the NDP came into power. He also served as legislative assistant to Premier Ed Schreyer during the early years of the MMF. Allard says the province was actively seeking out Métis people to form an organization. He says it was nothing more than an effort by government bureaucrats to create programs to be run by the Métis, which in turn would be run by the bureaucrats. The Métis would get some money. The bureaucrats would have lots of work to do overseeing the Métis-run programs. Of course, says Allard, it meant that the programs couldn't be too successful. If poor Métis no longer needed help, the programs would no longer be needed, and neither would the bureaucrats. Nonetheless, with the help of two government bureaucrats, the Manitoba Métis Federation was incorporated December 28, 1967. Ironically, the first directors were all Indians.

Adam Cuthand, a deacon of the Anglican church who'd had to give up his status to become a minister, became the first president. Joe Keeper, a community development worker who'd helped resettle the people of Moose Lake in Easterville after Moose Lake was flooded by Manitoba Hydro, was a director. (His later claim to fame is being the father of Tina Keeper, the star of CBC-TV's *North of Sixty*). The second director was the big, amiable Alfred Disbrowe from Berens River.

The MMF received a modest grant of $20,000 from the Manitoba government to set up a little office. The next step was to become a legitimate organization representing Métis people. After all, the MMF couldn't run programs if it didn't have a formal structure and a way of being connected to the people it represented. Or at least, the appearance of being connected. In 1969, the MMF represented only the 20 people who'd created it. That's when Stan Fulham came into the picture.

Fulham, in full uniform, was sitting in the restaurant in the Marlborough Hotel in Winnipeg, contemplating his pending retirement from the Royal Canadian Air Force. At an adjacent table sat Adam Cuthand and Angus Spence, trying to figure out how to go about creating a constitution for the MMF, something neither of them had any experience with. Fulham says they struck up a conversation, as people sometimes do in restaurants, and by the time they parted company, Spence and Cuthand had offered to pay him $700 a month to organize the MMF. Fulham says he didn't know much about constitution writing either, but he was game. He called on Dale Gibson, the dean of the law school at the University of Manitoba, for advice. "There was no money for consultants. Dale agreed to go through the law library and flag areas related to constitutions. I couldn't go there on weekdays because of the students, so I spent three weekends there studying constitutional law."[4]

Little Empires

Fulham worked out the constitutional draft, then divided the province into five regions, with the idea that two people representing each region would help work on the constitution and structure of the organization.

That's when he spotted the MMF's biggest flaw—the polarization of regional interests. "I could see problems with too much regionalization. I said we should have a provincial board. We'd have a conference with about a hundred people and we'd elect the best six or eight people. We wanted people who could see the bigger issues, work on the issues at the provincial or national level. But I was already too late."[5]

The people representing the regions on the initial board were digging in on the issue of control. They wanted each of the regions to have control of its own area and the money to run the regional office, and they wanted each to operate autonomously. The regional representatives didn't want control in the hands of a single provincial board. The tantalizing vision of little regional empires had firmly taken hold. And there was more money. The federal government was now in the funding act. The Secretary of State was providing $45,000, and offering more.

Fulham, Spence and Ferdinand Guiboche were invited to Ottawa to meet with Secretary of State Robert Stanbury in the spring of 1971. The fledgling Métis groups from Alberta and Saskatchewan were there, too. Fulham says Stanbury was offering lots of money, but the Manitoba delegation was worried. "Maybe I'm cynical," Fulham said, "but I figured if the government was giving out money, they'd be wanting something in return. Angus thought if we got too much money, he said then you'd have all this in-fighting over money. He said maybe we should do without government money. Make do with what we can do on our own. Ferdinand agreed."[6]

Core Funding

Fulham says the initial board was well aware of the dangers of accepting core funding from any government. He says Spence always referred to core funding as "political funding." "We spent hours, sometimes days, in philosophical debates over whether we should be taking government money for anything but programs. Angus felt program funding was different, but depending on government for the money to run the basic operation was dangerous."[7]

The board did finally opt for accepting core funding from the province, but only because they felt they had no choice. The people the MMF was organized to represent were the poor Métis. The board agreed that those people could not pay the kind of membership fees needed to keep the MMF independent of government. The Manitoba delegation knew they were going to have to take money from the Secretary of State. In the end, they decided maybe another $35,000 on top of the $65,000 they were already getting would be enough to run the office and some programs. Stanbury gave them an additional $125,000. He insisted.

Fulham says it was strictly political. The Secretary of State was paying out a lot of money to fund Indian organizations, and it wouldn't have looked good not to be supporting other aboriginal groups. "I was sitting on my hotel balcony that night," says Fulham, "and Ferdinand came in. He said this is the worst thing that could happen to Métis people. All it's going to do is lead to fighting."[8]

By November of 1971, the constitution proposing the provincial board had been drafted and locals were being set up in Métis communities across the province. The president, vice-president and secretary from each local were invited to the constitutional meeting in The Pas, with the MMF paying their expenses. Fulham says they'd all had a chance to go over the proposed constitution, and he felt most people supported the provincial board concept. Allan Ross from Norway House chaired the meeting. Fulham was taking minutes. As a staff person, he wasn't allowed to speak at the meeting, and couldn't defend the provincial board concept.

Fulham says even though a number of the initial board members had said they'd oppose regional control, no one did. The regional forces, led by Guiboche, won the day, and the constitution was amended to elect a vice-president and two directors from each region. They would also make up the provincial board. That, of course, meant each regional group would be championing its own interests instead of the interests of the organization as a whole. Fulham was deeply disappointed. "I said to Angus after the meeting, 'this organization is going to be in big trouble.'" The battle for control of the MMF began at that meeting, and it's never ended.

The die had been cast. The MMF was taking government money,

people had jobs and offices to run, and now the directors had to worry about keeping the money flowing. That begat the first big lie. "We used to say there were all these Métis people in Manitoba," says Fulham, "but when we started, we really didn't know. When I travelled around the province setting up locals, I realized there weren't 200,000 or 100,000. Maybe not even 20,000. Maybe only 10,000. And those were not good numbers."

Since the amount of funding provided by the government generally depends on the size of the constituency being served, the MMF didn't want the government to know how few poor and needy Métis there really were. So the MMF started publishing the *Manitoba Métis Federation News*, a broadsheet put out occasionally, but filled with newsy items about MMF activities. Fulham says it was intended to make the Métis community look larger and busier than it really was. "It's like the Wizard of Oz. Like this big voice representing hundreds of thousands of Métis, but there was really only us. I didn't care if the Métis read the paper. I was putting it out for the government bureaucrats.[9]

Fulham says that's also why he wanted the MMF board to be elected by the three people from each local. "With those three [delegates], you gave the election credibility. If everyone was allowed to vote, the government would see only three or four thousand people were voting." Thus began the illusion of Métis numbers. Fulham says he suspected then-Premier Ed Schreyer had a pretty good idea of the real numbers, but never raised the issue. The provincial government also benefited from the illusion that program funding was helping a far larger number of people than actually existed. And the NDP was serving one of its largest constituencies—the aboriginal people of northern and central Manitoba. But the bureaucratic numbers games aside, there were plenty of Métis people in dire need of help.

It's not that the federal and provincial governments weren't doing anything. They were pumping millions of dollars into Manitoba under programs like the Local Employment Assistance Program (LEAP), Manpower Corps, Special ARDA (a government grant and loan program for Native people), Department of Regional Economic Expansion (DREE), Remote Housing, Newstart and half-a-dozen more. In a report prepared for the MMF in 1972, Stan Fulham wrote that he believed about 95 percent of the programs did little, if anything, to improve the lives of impoverished Native people.

The MMF targeted education in its first official program. It provided a $5,000 bursary fund for Métis students needing financial help to get through high school, and enough money to hire an education coordinator. Housing was the next program. By 1972, the MMF had housing committees in place in Métis communities to help decide where limited financial resources would go. The Canada Mortgage and Housing Corporation was providing $300,000 for housing repairs, and that allowed the hiring of housing staff in each of the regions.

But Spence was worried about creating Métis ghettos. He wondered if repairing and building houses for people in places where they had little hope of decent employment wasn't doing a great disservice to Métis people. Spence wanted housing programs directed to needy Métis in Winnipeg, too. He knew from first-hand experience how little help was available to Métis who had migrated to the province's largest city. Spence never made any secret of the fact that when he'd arrived in Winnipeg in the 1950s, he'd faced discrimination in housing and employment. And then he took the route followed by too many uprooted Métis. He fell inside a bottle, and didn't come out until he woke one morning lying in a city gutter, covered with lice. He joined Alcoholics Anonymous and became a staunch supporter of the organization.

One of the more significant reports to come out of the MMF in the early years was a proposal called "In Search of a Future." It was written by Stan Fulham in 1972. Rather than attempt to keep poor Métis people locked in their communities, the report acknowledged that with few resources and few employment opportunities in remote rural areas, the best way to assist Métis in bettering their lives was to assist them in migrating to urban centres like Winnipeg. Like Chretien's White Paper promoting assimilation, the report pointed out the fruitlessness of spending large amounts of money on training and economic development programs that were destined to collapse the minute government money stopped flowing. The report proposed setting up migration centres to help Métis make the transition to an urban lifestyle. The MMF didn't get the funding for the proposal, but it did later set up a short-lived transition centre in Thompson.

The MMF had been set up to run programs for government, and it was running them. Just not very well. In the summers of 1969 and 1970, a hundred houses were to be built in ten remote Métis communities where welfare was the main source of income. The MMF set up housing committees to select who would receive the ten houses in each of the communities. The project was being funded by the province through the

Manitoba Housing and Renewal Corporation. A former housing worker says the opportunity of getting a house set neighbour against neighbour. He says as long as everyone was equally poor, neighbours were generous in sharing their limited resources. But as soon as some were offered more than others, jealousy reached a full boil. It didn't help, he says, that looking after family first meant the relatives and friends of the people on the MMF housing committee got first dibs on the new houses. And when construction workers were required, it mattered less if they knew anything about the building code or could tell one end of a hammer from another than if they were a needy relative of the MMF housing officer.

The project was disastrous. MHRC set the rules for the program, and officials insisted new houses be built together in rows. For Métis who lived on islands or in the bush well away from their neighbours, living cheek by jowl with other families (some of whom they might be feuding with) was not what they wanted. People complained that the houses were damp and mildewy. Nails popped out of walls, foundations shifted and walls cracked. And the houses weren't cheap. Someone had decided to build the new houses like it was a city street, and someone had decided to charge them high monthly payments. The Métis didn't distinguish between the MMF and the MHRC. They were perceived as one and the same. The Métis turned on the MMF for its lousy housing program, not realizing the government was pulling all the strings. The MMF ended up defending government bureaucrats to its members.

The MMF program to build city housing fared better, but it was overshadowed by the problems with other efforts. Joe Sawchuk, who had worked as a researcher on the housing program later wrote a 1980 report entitled "Development or Domination: the Métis and Government Funding." He pointed out that such programs do little to improve the lives of the people they're supposed to help. He noted that, similarly, the Special ARDA program intended to help native farmers was structured by government so that few, if any, people could qualify for loans. Again, Métis people got their hopes up that they'd get financial help, and again they were dashed. They blamed the MMF.

"The use of government subsidies and programs", wrote Sawchuk, "is a two-edged sword, for it cannot be said that the Métis have as yet achieved any real economic or political independence. In fact, they have managed to make themselves more dependent on government than ever before. The government, in supporting [the MMF], has a powerful club to hold over the

Métis. Any time the actions of the Federation do not please the government, funding can be withdrawn."

But even if the MMF had little control over the programs it was administering, it was at least providing employment. In poor rural communities, jobs with the MMF in housing or in the regional offices were highly sought after. Of course, getting the jobs often depended on having a family member in a position to do the hiring, and that power rested with the regional offices. The position of regional vice-president paid a nice salary with perks, and lots of jobs for the vice-president's family. Although the two directors from each region weren't on salary, they still had access to the perks and the power to employ their kin. But the vice-president and the directors had to be elected by the regional membership. It could have been a problem, except that the regions also had the authority to reject membership applications submitted by the locals. It helped ensure the "right" people stayed in control.

The MMF had become the Métis bureaucratic arm of the provincial NDP government and, to a lesser degree, the Liberal government in Ottawa. But the organization had become an economic development program itself, providing employment to those lucky (or clever) enough to get elected, or those lucky (or connected) enough to be hired as staff, consultants to write applications for more government money, consultants to research new programs which would need more government money and in turn would require more staff and consultants, and so on. The actual results of programs became moot. For example, the funding of bursaries to help Métis students through school was dropped in favour of funding research into acquiring more funding to hire consultants to set up a separate corporate structure with a board of directors and staff, which in turn would work on ways of funding bursaries to help Métis students through school. Instead of helping just one kid, the MMF could employ five or six people and receive an additional $300,000 from government.

The early years of MMF operations were fraught with botched attempts to actually deliver help to poor Métis, but at least the early leaders tried. "Big Ed" Head was elected MMF president in 1975, beating out 24-year-old Yvon Dumont. During his short term at the helm, Head tried to redirect the course of the MMF by breaking down the little regional empires. At the 1976 annual assembly, Head told delegates that he wanted to eliminate the salaried positions for the six vice-presidents (another region had been added). He said the regions were refusing to be accountable to head office for the funding they received, and when regional officials were asked for financial information, the told head office staff "to go to hell and mind their own business."[10]

That cost Head the election. The regional executives, who helped select the delegates to the assembly, had no intention of letting anyone tamper with their empires. The delegates elected the candidate who promised *more* control for the regions, John Morrisseau.

Morrisseau, a trapper and rancher from Crane River, took over the leadership of the MMF just in time for some of its most turbulent years, The annual budget had climbed to nearly $400,000, but the MMF was heavily in the red. To make matters worse, the MMF was no longer the administrative arm of Schreyer's NDP government. It was now dealing with a Conservative government led by the fiercely partisan Sterling Lyon. He did not look fondly upon the NDP creation. Morrisseau used an aggressive and confrontational style in dealing with government. Sometimes it worked. Sometimes it backfired.

SIT-INS AND BANNOCK

In the spring of 1979, Morrisseau led an MMF occupation of a Canada Manpower office in downtown Winnipeg. About 30 people staged a week-long sit-in to pressure the federal government for job creation guarantees for northern Manitoba. The protesters said they weren't leaving until they got an ironclad guarantee Ottawa would provide long-term jobs for the 66 percent unemployed among the province's 120,000 Métis.[11] Some media used a figure of 90 percent unemployment.

The battles fought by Louis Riel in the 1800s, said Morrisseau, weren't too different from the battles the Métis were fighting now. "He wanted to feed his people because his people were hungry.... We want jobs so we can feed our people. Things haven't changed that much."[12] After a week of dramatic headlines that hinted at the volatile presence of the militant American Indian Movement, the federal government "caved in" to MMF demands.

Was it real, or was it a staged event to allow the federal Liberals to rush to the aid of the poor Métis with millions of dollars of aid through programs like LEAP and Outreach programs?

The demonstration also served to reinforce the image of the MMF as an advocate for its people. If the MMF was not in conflict with government, at least once in a while, people might begin to figure out the MMF was more often than not serving the government.

If this was the tactic, it was hardly new. When courting Indian leaders, politicians knew they were dealing with people who had good reason to be suspicious of government, and it was necessary to reinforce a façade of friction between themselves and their chosen Indian organizations. "It was imperative that the Indian people unite behind their provincial associations," said native author Jim Burke,

> otherwise dissension and opposition would surface when these bodies began to enact government policies. But how to accomplish this, when these leaders had been sponsored and maintained by the government of which the Indians were, by nature, exceedingly suspicious?
>
> Indians, like most groups with a common bond, will readily band together against a common enemy. The Department of Indians Affairs (having a considerable head start) was set up as the villain against which the Indians could present a common front, behind their provincial leaders. Chretien's White Paper was intended as a straw man which the provincial leaders would—amid a storm of publicity—knock down, demonstrating to their constituents that they were a match for the federal government and able representatives of their people.[13]

"It was the biggest hypocrisy of all," says retired politician Jean Allard. "But the bureaucrats required that. They couldn't give out money without their going through these embarrassing scenes. It's all pre-arranged, just like all-star wrestling."[14] Smoke and mirrors. Wind and rabbit tracks.

Fresh from that successful Canada Manpower face-off with Ottawa, Morrisseau staged another sit-in, this time on the steps of the Manitoba Legislature. Morrisseau did nothing to endear himself to the Premier when national television camera crews showed up to film the poor starving Métis who were subsisting on only bannock and water under the hot summer sun. The issue was still jobs for the north, but Morrisseau was also demanding a cash infusion of $100,000 for the MMF, enough to pull the organization out of the red.

But it appears the legislature sit-in did not fit into the strategy of the provincial Tories. They weren't playing on the same team. Perhaps Morrisseau hoped to embarrass the Lyon government into a financial rescue for the MMF, but it didn't work. Lyon did negotiate more provincial funding for northern economic development. He dealt directly with the municipal governments, bypassing the MMF and its demonstrators as if they were of no consequence. Morrisseau was left with egg on his face. He finally told the Métis who had been demonstrating on the Legislative grounds for four weeks to go home. It was a sharp reminder of who was in charge of the game, and it wasn't Morrisseau.

The MMF's close alliance with the NDP undermined the organization. It wasn't surprising to find a Conservative-allied group threatening to split the MMF. A dissident group, led by MMF Dauphin vice-president Walter Menard, claimed the MMF no longer represented the Métis of Manitoba. "In the past, the MMF has been too occupied with its own administration to give representation to local people," said Menard. "At the moment, 85 to 95 percent of the MMF time and money goes into administration."[15] Menard formed the Métis Confederacy of Manitoba, claiming it would be the voice of the Métis of Manitoba. Menard retained his salaried position of MMF vice-president.

The Confederacy won political credibility almost immediately by winning Manitoba's two seats on the Native Council of Canada. Following a three-hour confrontation between the Confederacy and the Métis Federation at the annual meeting of the Native Council of Canada in Ottawa in August, 1979, the Confederacy was firmly endorsed as the political voice of the Métis in Manitoba. It wasn't as if the MMF couldn't have stayed on the national council. But in typical MMF fashion, it had gotten in a huff earlier over an internal dispute, taken its marbles and stormed off home, leaving two vacant council seats that the Confederacy was only too happy to fill.

The Confederacy was cementing its position as an alternative to the MMF. "The federation isn't doing the job it was set up for. The leaders are off on a tangent and don't seem to be able to stop," said Menard. "Over 12 years, it has evolved from several decentralized groups into one centrally controlled shop that's detrimental to the Métis people."[16] And certainly detrimental to the regional vice-presidents.

There was more trouble brewing in the South-west Region where MMF members were agitating against the entrenched control of the vice-president and his family. About 30 people marched in front of the MMF regional office in Brandon. Vern Kalmakoff, the chairman of the Grand Valley local, organized the protest against vice-president George Fleury. Fleury had been running the region from day one, and Kalmakoff accused him of building "a personal empire" by hiring family members for MMF jobs, and by refusing to explain items in the region's financial statements. His vocal criticism was not taken kindly. His MMF membership was revoked at an emergency regional meeting.

Fleury defended his actions, saying Kalmakoff had no concrete evidence to support his allegations. Fleury also said Kalmakoff's membership would not be restored until he proved himself worthy of being an MMF member. One of the Grand Valley local members said that was the same thing that had happened to Kalmakoff's predecessor who "was kicked out for no reason except that he was questioning what George Fleury was doing."[17]

The message was clear. To prove themselves worthy of being MMF members, Métis people had to support the existing regime.

FUNDING PULLED

With the MMF turning into a political nuisance, and a rival group with a more "conservative" bent on the scene, the Lyon government pulled all provincial funding for Métis groups and appointed an advisory group to study Métis funding policies. Morrisseau, along with the NDP members sitting in Opposition, accused Lyon of playing partisan politics because he saw the MMF as too closely aligned with the New Democrats. Lyon responded by accusing Morrisseau of staging publicity stunts to divert attention from the MMF's internal problems.

The MMF had lost annual provincial funding of $130,000, but it still had $500,000 coming from Ottawa. But the federal government wasn't very happy with the MMF either. At the same time the province withdrew its funding, federal Employment minister Lloyd Axworthy ordered a study into native employment programs in Manitoba. The three-person task force, headed up by consultant David Walker, roundly condemned the MMF's participation in programs like Outreach and LEAP. The report noted that the federal government's decision the previous fall to allow the

MMF virtual control over the $3 million allocated for Métis and non-status Indians "created considerable friction and has eventually threatened the legitimacy of LEAP."[18]

"The MMF does not have a history of successful management," the report continued, "nor does it have an economic development strategy or an administrative infra-structure to carry out an ambitious role in LEAP."[19] The report even questioned the MMF's legitimacy as a representative of the Métis people.

Morrisseau accused the federal government of striking back at the MMF for staging the sit-in at the Manpower office. "The only way they can come back at us is to punish us economically," he said. Morrisseau said the provincial government was trying to bring the MMF to its knees by withholding funding and organizing critical task forces.[20]

Politically speaking, the stage had been set for the demise of the MMF. An alternative group was in place, and there was enough bad publicity about the MMF to justify terminating all its funding. It was a salutary lesson for Morrisseau…you play the game or you're gone. By the fall of 1980, the president of the Confederacy was predicting the imminent collapse of the MMF. "I tend to think the MMF will cease to exist within the next two or three months, and that will be a whole lot better for the Métis people of Manitoba."[21]

Despite the MMF's shaky future, Morrisseau ran again for president in 1980, and was handily elected. The raucous three-day assembly ended with accusations of vote-buying and election fraud. Former president Angus Spence was at the assembly. He was not impressed with what he saw. "It is depressing to see what is happening to the organization," he told reporters.[22]

In February of the following year, the Conservative government finally released the advisory committee's report on funding of Métis groups. The report recommended that operating grants be given to the MMF. The Lyon government not only didn't restore the MMF's annual $130,000 grant, it ignored the recommendation of the advisory committee and vetoed any future payments to the group.

Morrisseau resigned, citing failing health. And the MMF survived, thanks to a provincial election that saw the return of the NDP to power. Morrisseau quickly recovered his health to take the position of deputy minister of Northern Affairs under the new government. Despite all the drama and publicity, the MMF was still small potatoes on the political scene. It wasn't until the Dumont years that the MMF hit the big time.

CHAPTER FIVE

THE DUMONT DYNASTY

Yvon Dumont was only 33 years old when he became president of the MMF in 1984, but he'd already put in 17 years in Métis politics. His first official position at the age of 16 was secretary-treasurer of the St. Laurent local, pre-dating the formalizing of the MMF structure. He was president of the high school Youth Club and served on student council as class representative, social representative and vice-president. At the same time, he was secretary-treasurer of the St. Laurent Recreation Committee.

Dumont had grown up with Métis politics for breakfast, lunch and supper. His father Willie had been one of the group of people who founded the MMF. As the community development worker in St. Laurent, Willie was involved in just about everything going on in the community. Yvon grew up in a large family, with five brothers and three sisters. Two other siblings died young. His father was involved in numerous entrepreneurial ventures, but his business tactics left some people unimpressed. His mother Therese, a devoutly religious woman widely admired by people in the community, was considered the strength of the family.

Yvon, say friends, inherited both his mother's work ethic and his father's interest in politics, and his ability to wheel and deal. "He was never a child," says a woman who grew up with Yvon. "He was always like a little grown-up." He had the ability to speak in front of a crowd. That made him a rarity amongst people who were often too shy, insecure and conscious of their lack of education to want to draw public attention to themselves. He was elected as a director of the MMF in 1971, and his political skills earned him a recommendation to the newly-formed Native Council of Canada. At

21, he moved to Ottawa to become the vice-president of the NCC.

That's where Dumont got his first close-up look at how the big boys play. Pierre Trudeau had been prime minister for four years, and Trudeaumania was waning. The introduction of the Official Languages Act, the fall-out from the FLQ crisis, the use of the War Measures Act in Québec, and constitutional wrangling over amendments to the British North America Act had taken of the bloom off the rose. But Trudeau was still a powerful political force. Dumont had little to do with Trudeau, but he did get a ringside seat watching the way powerful people operated. Friends say that's when he got his first taste of real power and real money.

But Dumont didn't stay in Ottawa. After a year, he resigned his position and moved back to St. Laurent. Friends say he was completely out of his element and terribly homesick. In 1973, he was again elected to the MMF board, and the next year took over the newly-created position of executive vice-president. Dumont's taste for politics led him to run for the St. Laurent municipal council in 1983. But he hadn't been on council long before he was charged with stealing Christmas trees.

"In December of 1983," said Dumont, "a friend of mine and I decided that we would take our kids out looking for Christmas trees, and we wanted to find some Crown land nearby that had Christmas trees on them. And we wanted to go out in the bush like there are stories written about, with our children and cut down some Christmas trees and bring them home for Christmas."[1]

They ended up on private land, and were confronted by the farmer who owned the land just as they finished strapping three or four trees on the top of their station wagon. Dumont said they offered to pay the farmer for them, but were refused. As they were driving home, they were pulled over by the RCMP. The police had just received a call from the farmer reporting the theft of Christmas trees. Dumont explained that they thought the trees were on public land, but unfortunately, they hadn't bothered to get a permit to cut down trees on Crown land, either.

Dumont and his friend were charged with theft of property over $200. They appeared in court in Lundar early in 1984 and pleaded not guilty. They weren't convicted. The Crown ended up dropping the charges because of lack of evidence.

Dumont was not happy with the decision, and how it reflected on his political image.

It was embarrassing for us to have to go and stand before a packed courtroom of people who know us and have a charge read out saying that we were charged with theft of property of a value over $200, and then for the Crown prosecutor to say that they recommended the case be dismissed because they didn't have the evidence. That didn't mean that we were not guilty to a lot of people that were standing in the courtroom. It meant that we got away with it.[2]

Dumont blamed the incident on racial discrimination. He said he and his friend were charged because they were Métis. And there were racial tensions in St. Laurent. The village was in the midst of a development boom. Perched on the edge Lake Manitoba, and only 80 kilometres northwest of Winnipeg, it was an ideal location for a summer cottage community. Within a few short years, the limited beachfront property was snapped up, and the summer population boomed. The cottagers wanted to keep the beach-front to themselves. The locals still wanted access to the lake on hot summer days, but they were being restricted to a tiny public beach or the long sweep of undeveloped beachfront about 10 kilometres from town. The only way to get to that stretch of beach was by a single narrow road with the beach-front cottages on one side and the vast Lake Francis swamp on the other.

What got the cottagers' backs up most was the presence of the Los Bravos biker gang. St. Laurent was home to a large number of gang members, and home to the Bravos' annual summer celebration. Hundreds of bikers turned up for the weekend party, roaring down the single road past the cottages to the undeveloped beach. It would be something of an understatement to say the cottagers were uncomfortable with so many bikers in full colours having a heck of a good time just a hop, skip and jump down the beach. They complained to the municipal council, but the councillors weren't about to close off the beach to local people who also happened to be Bravos. It was inevitable that there would be confrontations between the partiers and cottagers. After a particularly vicious assault on a cottager, other cottage owners let it be known they were arming themselves.

There were complaints about the police's inability to keep law and order in St. Laurent. One officer said, "RCMP cannot use brute force to keep youths in line because the police are outnumbered, and the youths are impervious to threats and reasoning. I wouldn't own a cottage there on a bet. There really is a wild bunch out there."[3]

There were three power structures in St. Laurent—the municipal council, the local MMF association and the Los Bravos. With the overlap of membership between the Bravos and the MMF, a public perception developed that the biker gang was the enforcement arm of the MMF. Several people in St. Laurent still bear the scars of "an attitude adjustment" courtesy of a couple of burly bikers. (When asked for interviews, they were quite adamant that it was healthier all around not to dredge up old history.)

There is no evidence to support the idea that Los Bravos acted in any kind of official capacity for the MMF, either in St. Laurent or Winnipeg. Most of the linkage between the Bravos and the MMF appears to be through family relationships. The dark spectre of the biker gang did, however, find its way into election campaigns and financial deals. It helped sway uncooperative people if they were reminded who had cousins and in-laws in the Bravos. Fear is a great motivator. Actual assaults by gang members appear to have been done to help out family and friends. Nonetheless, the threat of a visit by Los Bravos continues to be invoked as an intimidation tactic. (Los Bravos heavy-weight Pat Coutu actually ran for a council seat in St. Laurent in 1989. He won by acclamation, since no one ran against him. Coutu wasn't in office long. Perhaps he was quickly bored by the endless discussions of grader blade purchases and culvert sizes, but he quit showing up for meetings. After he violated the Municipal Act by missing three meetings in a row, council was able to quietly terminate his position.)

A Dynasty Begins

Yvon Dumont was serving as the electoral officer for the 1984 MMF election. He told friends that as he'd gone around to various communities setting up the election, people had been telling him he should run for office.

The president's position paid $40,000 a year. Dumont had a family to support, and the president's salary was far more than he could make cutting wood or driving for a Winnipeg courier service.

Don McIvor had just finished an unremarkable three-year tenure, and was running again. One of the major changes McIvor had instituted was a one-person, one-vote policy for elections. The idea was being pushed by the Métis Confederacy, but McIvor said he supported the idea as well. The Confederacy was making conciliatory noises. The Métis needed to speak with one voice, said Confederacy leaders, and if the MMF went along with changing the election process, they would consider dissolving. The Métis Confederacy officially dissolved in 1984.

MMF finances were helped during McIvor's tenure when the New Democrats were returned to power in Manitoba under Premier Howard Pawley. Provincial funding was restored.

The MMF had filed a lawsuit against the Province of Manitoba and the Government of Canada claiming the land provisions of the Manitoba Act in 1870 had not been fulfilled. Ottawa had been giving the MMF money to research the land claim since 1976, and a lawsuit was filed in 1981. The case was halted two years later when the Manitoba government promised to participate in talks to reach an out of court settlement. The Pawley government was not backing the MMF's land claim, and the issue created a rift between the political allies. "We are satisfied as a government that there is no legal liability on our part with respect to the claims," stated the provincial Attorney General.[4]

"We went out on a limb to support this NDP to get into power..." said former president Ed Head. "But these people don't make any commitments. They tell us they have an open door policy, but when you walk inside the door you see the cupboards are empty."[5]

Political times were changing. Trudeau's tired Liberals were facing an election, and a fresh-faced Brian Mulroney had just wrested the Conservative party leadership from Joe Clark.

And there was Yvon Dumont, sensing a chance to take over the leadership of the MMF. Mid-campaign, he advised the MMF board he was adding his name to the ballot for president, and the job of running the election was turned over to Jean Allard. Dumont won the vote handily. "There have been a lot of political problems within the organization," said the victorious Dumont. "My object will be to get locals and regions working together as a team."[6]

Unlike earlier presidents, Dumont wasn't about to spend his time haggling with provincial bureaucrats for a few thousand dollars here and there. He knew the real power and money were in the hands of the big boys in Ottawa. In 1985, Dumont reactivated the land claims case. Tom Berger agreed to take on the case, warning Dumont that the MMF had to be prepared to take it all the way to the Supreme Court of Canada. He also warned Dumont against being in too a big a hurry to spend the money expected from a settlement. "I think it would be unwise for the Métis to allow their heads to be turned by the suggestion that billions of dollars may be obtained," Berger wrote in a letter to Dumont. "What is at stake here is a land claim. The vital thing is to get the federal government and the province to come to terms with the Métis land claim. As Prime Minister Mulroney said at the Constitutional Conference earlier this year, the Métis are entitled to a 'land base.'"

In fact, winning the lawsuit would only establish that the governments of Canada and Manitoba failed to carry out the land settlement promised in the Manitoba Act. That, in turn, would be used in a later action against the governments to determine a settlement made up, perhaps, of land and money to compensate for losses.

In 1985, the MMF was still in the red, but as the executive director reported, "Despite the lack of resources, both human and financial, we have continued to grow in strength and numbers. Some of those persons who in the past have 'wandered' towards other organizations are now seeking membership again within the Manitoba Métis Federation."[7]

The MMF was still in the housing business, delivering the Rural and Native Housing program for all of rural Manitoba, not just the Métis communities. Each of the regional offices had one housing development officer, but a lack of resources meant most other housing staff had to be laid off. The publishing arm of the MMF, renamed Pemmican Publications, had about 35 books and booklets available, including the popular *In Search of April Raintree* by Beatrice Culleton. But it was constantly struggling to find enough money to pay the bills. The child and family services workers in each region were limited to the role of monitoring referrals in their respective areas, but it was seen as a small step toward a full-fledged Métis child care agency.

For the first time, the Métis had their own pavilion at Folklorama. The Métis Women's Alliance was formed. Angus Spence was awarded the first Aboriginal Order of Canada by the Native Council of Canada. He died in the summer of 1985.

The regional offices were grumbling about the lack of money coming their way, and the lack of attention from head office. The Interlake region vice-president Al Chartrand made his opinion clear at the 1985 annual assembly.

We, the Métis, have not been given the chance to take part or been made to feel that we belong to the Manitoba Métis Federation, although we are sure looked at when to comes to voting in an election. One of the biggest concerns I have is with the annual assemblies that the MMF has had every year. The MMF spends between $80,000 to $100,000 a year on the annual assembly. If we are so interested in doing something for ourselves and our children, we should divide that money between the regions and let the locals have the money so we can build a stronger region, not play with the money as we are doing.

That idea didn't get very far. Money was still short, but Dumont had plans. He'd already been to Ottawa.

MULRONEY DISCIPLE

Much of Dumont's political success can be attributed to being in the right place at the right time. A few months after Dumont took over the MMF, Brian Mulroney's Conservatives were elected to office in Ottawa. At the same time, the Indians were becoming more and more vocal in their criticism of federal government policy. Ottawa was losing control over the Indian voices they had created in the 1960s. The Indians no longer needed to play ball with federal politicians because they had so much public support and sympathy, they knew Ottawa wouldn't dare pull the financial plug on their organizations. That meant they were free to bite the hand feeding them and not lose any funding.

What Ottawa needed was an aboriginal voice they could still control. Someone who could throw aboriginal support behind whatever government policy was being floated. After all, most of the public still didn't know the difference between Indians and Métis, and they could easily interpret Métis support as Indian support. Brian Mulroney found a willing disciple in Yvon Dumont.

Dumont didn't plan on spending his time bickering with the MMF vice-presidents over who should be in control of the regions. He was quite happy to dole out the regions' share of government funding and let them do with it as they pleased. He was after programs and government funding that could be controlled from his office. When Dumont became MMF president in 1984, the federal and provincial governments were providing funding of $873,000. By 1992, Dumont's hard work was paying off. The two levels of government were kicking in funding to the tune of nearly $4 million.

CHAPTER SIX

MORE MONEY

Yvon Dumont wasn't spending much time at home with his family by 1992. He was too busy trying to keep control of the MMF and its more than two dozen subsidiary corporations, and fighting off the regional vice-presidents and directors who wanted more of the big bucks he was bringing in. The MMF wasn't just a vehicle to transfer money to the seven regional corporations anymore. (Winnipeg was finally given its own regional office.) The head office was retaining control of big-dollar programs like housing. The regions might each have their own housing officers and field staff, but they were hired and paid through head office.

On paper, the regions still had control of the MMF. Each region contributed one vice-president and two directors to the board, accounting for 21 positions. The Métis women's group held another seat. Dumont occupied the president's chair. Since Dumont cast only one of 23 votes around the board table, the regional vice-presidents should have been able to carve up all the head office programs without any difficulty. The majority of directors were from the regions, and well away from the head office in Winnipeg. Those directors worked out of Thompson, Brandon and The Pas. They didn't get to Winnipeg very often, and it was more difficult for them to keep tabs on what was going on in head office. The directors from the South-east, Winnipeg, Dauphin and Interlake regional offices were closer to the action. They appear to have cooperated in keeping control centred in Winnipeg; indeed, they occupied most of the key board positions of MMF subsidiary company like Manitoba Métis Community Investments Inc. and the Métis Housing Construction Corporation.

Some directors complained they didn't know what was going on, so they responded by setting up an array of committees. They needed committee meetings, said the directors, because it was the only way they could find out what was going on with all the MMF programs. For serving on these committees, they voted themselves a per diem of $200.

By 1992, the MMF head office was funding the meetings of nine committees, with the directors sharing 35 committee positions amongst themselves. If each of the committees got together for one meeting a month, it would amount to $84,000 extra tax-free dollars in the directors' pockets over and above the money they were already earning. The regional directors were collecting the per diem out of the head office budget, not their own. The directors who had been kept on the outside were telling Dumont that if he wasn't going to share information and resources willingly, they'd take what they considered their due some other way.

And the per diems were adding up. Board members were also collecting per diems for attending regular board meetings. One of the head office staff had the responsibility of making sure the per diems were paid out in cash at the end of a meeting. The MMF 1991/92 budget allowed for $7,500 in per diems for each day, just for board meetings. The annual assembly per diems totaled about $20,000 a day. At one meeting, a motion to suspend committees didn't even get a seconder. Why would any director support cutting off such a nice addition to their incomes?

Dumont's concern appears to have been both to prevent the committees from having too much power, and possibly take over control of the head office programs, as well as to stop a drain of financial resources.

Finally, in the summer of 1992, he did order a stop to committee meetings, a move he called "draconian" but necessary. The head office was experiencing severe cash flow problems. "By virtue of the foregoing," he said in a memo to directors and staff, "I am suspending, until further notice, any committee meetings or travel. In particular, travel requires my express approval or must be for emergent (sic) purpose. No travel for committee meetings or other expenses will be honoured by us during this period of time that we are in this cash flow problem."[1]

THE TAX MAN COMETH

In 1991, finance chairman Elbert Chartrand suggested to his committee that instead of the directors collecting a per diem every time they attended a meeting, they would be paid $500 a month as a directors' fee. That would also cover the per diems paid for regular board meetings. Expenses like travel, hotel rooms, meals and mileage would be claimed separately. The idea looked favourable for the directors. They would get the money whether they attended committee meetings or not. And from a head office point of view, it would be a way to control the amount of money being paid out in per diems and at the same time, take away some of the incentive for inquisitive directors to keep calling committee meetings.

What if, suggested some committee members, the $500 was paid on a separate check and not added to their normal payroll? "This allotment is taxable," warned Chartrand. "If this is not done, it's quite possible that the Receiver General Auditor can check *all* prior records. This could cause a great deal of problems for the Federation and for those who did not claim this as income. It is something to think about."[2] The finance committee took the idea to the next regular board meeting where it was promptly thrown out.

CORE FUNDING

The day-to-day operations of the MMF are paid for by core funding from government. Ottawa kicked in $531,555 for the year ending March 31, 1992. The Province of Manitoba added $218,400. The head office also collected an administrative fee and rent from its housing, tripartite and child and family services programs. That added another $149,000 to core funding. Add the $704,000 "profit" from the housing branch and a few special grants, and the tally hits $1.7 million.

A million of that was paid to the regional offices, the rest used by the head office. It may sound like a lot of money, but 75 percent of the core budget was used to pay salaries and benefits, per diems, travel expenses, meeting costs and travel allowances. The remaining 25 percent paid for the heat, lights, insurance, telephone, equipment purchases and other costs associated with running an office.

Since the regional offices are not accountable to the head office for how they spend the core money they get, regional expenses are not listed in the annual MMF financial statements. However, copies of regional financial statements indicate the same breakdown of core funding—75 percent for salaries, travel, meetings and benefits like meals and babysitting and 25 percent for actual office expenses. The head office salaries weren't outrageous. Yvon Dumont had a salary of $62,500. The general manager, Ed Swain, was collecting $63,600, Dumont's principle secretary Billyjo Delaronde was making $44,000. The women on the secretarial staff were getting an average of $12,000-$15,000.

But the MMF was very generous with staff perks. Staff were paid a $125 per diem for out-of-province travel. If anyone was required to be away from the office on business for more than four hours, the MMF picked up the tab for all meals. And some staff were paid just to go to work. They collected $60 a month to cover the costs of driving from their Winnipeg home to their Winnipeg workplace. (That amount was later increased to $125 per month.)

Yvon Dumont also got paid to drive to work. Since he lived in St. Laurent and had to commute all the way to Winnipeg, he was paid mileage to and from work. He also collected $125 a month for driving in the city. For the ten weeks from the beginning of February 1992 until mid-April, Dumont billed the MMF just over $2,400 for mileage, meals and per diems. Some weeks were less. Some were more.

An interim management audit conducted in 1993 when Ernie Blais became president noted that "the MMF does contribute substantial amounts to restaurants in this city. I note, particularly, that Alycia's Restaurant just down the street from the MMF is a popular eating place for staff members." The MMF, in these cases, was picking up the tab.

In the summer of 1992, general manager Ed Swain and his wife went on an all-expenses-paid, fact-finding mission to Norway and Sweden. The purpose, according to the two-page report he filed on return was "to make contact with the Sami People of Norway and Sweden for the purpose of self-government initiatives." The three-week trip cost the MMF $4,573.

The spending by MMF directors and staff on food and drink was often under attack. One disgruntled vice-president made public a hotel bill run up during an annual assembly by the Thompson region after he was suspended by Dumont for not calling a regional meeting. The hotel bill included a 17-

day liquor bill totaling $1,865. Bill Flamand, the Thompson vice-president, said he didn't consider the bill excessive. He said the other six regions opened hospitality suites and ran up similar tabs for entertaining delegates.[3]

There were perks for the secretarial staff, too, most of whom were single parents. Anyone who had to work late or on weekends, could collect up to $30 a day to cover baby-sitting expenses. The MMF was also very generous about giving out personal loans to staff and MMF members, and they were often not paid back. They'd just be written off as bad debts. In one year, the MMF wrote off 75 percent of its outstanding loans.

A study of personal loans issued by the MMF was conducted as part of an internal audit conducted in 1993 by Florence Matthews, Q.C. She noted that loans were being made without proper documentation, and there appeared to be no policy on charging interest or administrative fees. Some loans were interest-free with no administrative charge. Others were charged interest rates that varied between one percent and 27 percent. One person paid a $35 fee on a $3,000 loan, while another person paid a $150 fee for a $2,000 loan. In some cases, the paperwork on loans had simply disappeared.[4] The same report noted the MMF was having some trouble keeping track of the equipment it was buying. "In one instance, a staff member authorized the purchase of a computer and printer which were delivered directly to the member's residence for his family's use."[5] Continuing its generosity to staff and directors, the MMF also paid parking tickets and even covered the cost of a car rental for a staff member while he was vacationing in Las Vegas.

But not everyone had access to the MMF's largess. You had to be an elected director or a staff member to tap into the goodies. For many Métis whose life outside the MMF was circumscribed by poverty and isolation, being elected to office (or having a friend in office) was a rare opportunity to cash in on the good life—at least for a little while.

The staff of the MMF was highly politicized, and people who didn't toe the line were quickly shown the door. Everybody had a sister or son who needed a job or a friend who was owed a favour. Jobs could disappear in a flash.

Seasoned staffers learned to protect their jobs by putting the photocopier to good use. One woman admitted she routinely took documents off peoples' desks when no one was around, copied them and then put them back. She said she often had no idea if what she was taking was of any significance. She was looking for incriminating documents that might prove embarrassing to people like Dumont or Swain if they attempted to get rid of her. No one trusted anyone. Too much material was being spirited out of the office that could be used both to protect jobs, or to manipulate an election. And everyone suspected everyone else of doing the same thing.

Keeping Secrets

The MMF was running the head office with a budget of just under $1 million in 1992. The head office transferred another million dollars to the regional offices for administration costs, but it had to be split seven ways. The budgets ranged from $118,000 for the Winnipeg regional office (not to be confused with the MMF head office in Winnipeg) to $169,000 for the Thompson office. Head office no longer interfered in regional operations by requiring the regional vice-presidents to account for the money they were getting, but it seemed that the directors were eyeing all the goodies head office was keeping to itself.

Dumont had done a good job finding more government money during his years as president. He focused his attentions and talents on finding new ways to tap into government coffers with, as always, the willing assistance of government bureaucrats. The MMF had no other source of income. Every penny it spent came from public funds. So if it were to grow, it had to be with more government money.

Lucrative Deal

The MMF's most lucrative money-maker was the MMF housing branch. The MMF had been involved in housing programs of one sort or another since the early years, but they usually ended up being a colossal headache for both the MMF and the people on the receiving end of the programs. So many people who'd gotten involved in some of the earlier housing programs were facing eviction that former president Ed Head was hired by CMHC to help counsel families in financial distress. They couldn't afford the high payments of the new houses they'd been provided with, and complained of interior walls running with moisture, foundations shifting and cracking, and doors freezing shut in the winter. One frustrated housing worker in Norway House finally organized a mass eviction protest. In response to the litany of complaints, CMHC officials promised to provide money for *more* (my italics) housing programs.[6]

Under Dumont's administration, the glitches that had made running government housing programs so awkward were ironed out. The MMF had developed a more comfortable fit with the bureaucracy so that the money and paperwork flowed with greater ease. They'd learned to work as one.

The MMF's role in housing programs was to find needy families, apply to the appropriate CMHC or MHRC program on their behalf, and then hire the companies needed to complete the approved repairs or construction. For this, the federal and provincial governments covered all the costs of repairs and paid the MMF housing branch a most generous management fee. The more needy families who were processed by the housing staff, the more money the housing branch collected. And since the MMF was running housing programs for all of rural Manitoba, it didn't matter if the families were Métis or not.

Two vice-presidents got into an argument at a board meeting, says a former secretary, over who worked the hardest for the MMF. The dispute was settled by comparing the dollar value of the housing programs in each region. The winner had generated more income for the housing branch. The fact that the region had also supplied more improved housing for poor people did not appear to be the point. The vice-presidents were arguing over who should take credit for doing the most to bring in money for the MMF.

In 1992, the housing branch was running six government programs that raked in revenues of just over $1.7 million. Out of that, the housing branch paid half a million dollars in salaries and benefits to the housing staff, and used another $425,000 to cover office expenses, travel costs, consultants reports, furniture purchases, etc. That left $800,000 after expenses, a 90 percent surplus.

The profit from the housing branch was simply transferred to the MMF head office. It was understood that the excess housing branch revenues were to become part of the MMF's core funding. "In addition to fulfilling the desires of the membership for the Métis involvement in housing," reads a report prepared by the Housing Branch for the December finance committee meeting, "it happens to generate a great deal of revenues to assist in sustaining the other less financially profitable but just as valid activities of the Manitoba Métis Federation.... The branch proposes to generate a greater ratio of profits to expenditures given the shrinking budgets of government departments."[7] In other words, it was politically more acceptable for the government to disguise core funding as management fees paid through the housing branch.

According to internal financial records, the housing branch transferred $704,000 to the core funding account for the year ending March 31,1992. Of course, that was on paper. Staff say as fast as money came into the housing branch from the feds or the province it was transferred to the MMF account. And sometimes MMF expenses were just paid directly out of housing. In terms of bookkeeping, the lines between the housing branch and the head office were often blurred. That could explain why the housing branch was paying fees to a consultant hired to work for the Métis National Council as a liaison with the Prime Minister's Office, $1,600 to artist Marcien Le May for a model of a new Louis Riel statue, funding for the Métis Pavilion at Folklorama, the costs of an MMF board meeting, and a $6,000 loan to Billyjo Delaronde the week of his wedding.

In 1993 and 1994 and 1994, the housing branch generated gross revenues of $2.1 million and $2.4 million respectively. But the MMF waas short of money. Spending had gotten out of hand in anticipation of the huge land claims settlement. In 1993, the MMF board bled the housing branch account dry by transferring a total of $1.6 million into the general account. That left housing with a deficit of half a million dollars. The following year, the housing branch had to cover the short-fall, but stll managed to make a profit of just under a million dollars for the MMF.

Dreaming of Self-government

Dumont's second most lucrative deal was an agreement with Ottawa and the Manitoba government to fund exploration of Métis self-government in education, housing, economic development, child and family services and a data base. The goal of the agreement signed in 1989, was "designed to carry out the research, design and development of Métis institutions and negotiation of tripartite self-government agreements on a non-constitutional basis. The officials' role...is to address issues of jurisdiction, legislative authority, powers, fiscal resources and devolution of authority."[8]

In other words, a raft of staff and consultants would write a lot of reports proposing how the MMF could take over and run the five designated areas on behalf of the Métis of Manitoba. The agreement specifically stated the funding was to be used to study self-government, not to implement it. Neither could the funding be used for anything other than office expenses, salaries, committee meetings, consultants' fees, and travel expenses. For this, Ottawa and the Manitoba governments were paying a total of $630,000 annually. By 1992, the MMF had spent nearly $2 million dollars on reports developing MMF-controlled programs that would all require massive infusions of more government money. Some called for the provincial government to pass legislation to create an MMF-controlled institution of education (and proposed taking over an entire northern school division). One called on Ottawa to guarantee that an unspecified portion of federal procurement contracts be awarded, untendered, to yet-to-be-created Métis businesses. Then, once a year or so, Dumont would get together with Justice Minister Kim Campbell and provincial Northern Affairs minister Jim Downey and review the progress of report-writing.

Dumont, who chaired the tripartite committee, was also involved as president of the Métis National Council in creating the Métis Accord. The Accord covered constitutional changes necessary for Métis self-government, while the tripartite report-writing dealt with the nitty-gritty of instituting self-government in reality. Of course, it was all in the idea stage. But there was plenty of work to be had for report writers.

Another government offering was the provincial funding for the child and family services branch. The Manitoba government provided an annual grant of $215,000 to pay for a staff person in each regional office. Their job was to provide support services for Métis people dealing with the province's department of Child and Family Services and other government social services agencies.

GETTING INTO BANKING

Another jewel in Dumont's crown was the creation of the Louis Riel Capital Corporation. Ottawa had money available to set up aboriginal capital corporations to finance business development and investment in aboriginal businesses. LRCC was going to get $8.2 million in funding: $7.6 million for capitalization, $500,000 for administration costs and a $100,000 startup fee. Its mandate was to provide loans and loan guarantees to Métis business people who were eligible for membership in the MMF.

Ottawa was monitoring this program particularly carefully. The MMF wasn't going to be running the bank. Under the agreement, only two of the seven board positions could be filled by a board member or employee of the MMF or any of its affiliates. However, the MMF-controlled Manitoba Métis Community Investments Inc. (MMCII) was to be in charge of screening candidates for directors, and overseeing the operations of LRCC.

Even with some restrictions on direct MMF involvement, some people had serious doubts about the arrangement. Aboriginal activist Winnie Giesbrecht called it a Pandora's box. "No government should put a lending institution like this under the control of a political organization like the MMF. It's just common sense."[9] She said the capital corporation was an easy target for abuse, and she doubted MMF leaders could be stopped from influencing loan decisions. Dumont promised there would be no favouritism shown, and a government bureaucrat offered assurances that "stringent measures" were in place to prevent conflict of interest.

The MMF would have liked to have full control, but Dumont still appeared with Small Business minister Tom Hockin at a press conference to accept the deal on behalf of all Métis people.

Perhaps because of the limited involvement of the MMF, LRCC was considered one of the best-run aboriginal capital corporations in the country. But at the time of this writing, the chairman had resigned over an apparent dispute with MMF directors who were attempting a hostile takeover of LRCC operations.

The Losers

During Dumont's years as MMF president, it was inevitable he'd have a few financial stinkers. In fact, most of the MMF-sponsored business ventures were big money losers.

The MMF set up MMCII in 1984 to make investments that would give the MMF some income that wasn't controlled by government. The insiders knew the MMF was really a house of cards that could come tumbling down the minute either level of government found it politically expedient to pull their funding. MMCII didn't actually do any business until 1991 when the

Native Economic Development Program came through with $275,000 to start a construction company. That company would then be hired by the Housing Branch to do construction work and repairs authorized by CMHC/MHRC housing programs. The construction company tendered and built 16 houses and a special native women's transition centre in the first two years. The contracts were worth about $2 million. Unfortunately, the construction company didn't make a penny of profit. But the Native Economic Development Program came up with more money. It gave MMCII nearly a million dollars to build a 31,000 square foot office and warehouse in Winnipeg. The balance of the $1.8 million cost was financed with a mortgage from Peace Hills Trust.

The building was supposed to produce revenue for the MMF through rental income, but rental space often sat empty. MMCII had taken over another MMF money loser, Kingo. The St. Laurent company was started by MMF directors in 1989 as 2381576 Manitoba Ltd. to study and develop a processing plant for fish species generally not wanted on the local fish market but possibly wanted in Asian markets. Robert Gaudry was president of Kingo. He also sat as vice-president of the Interlake region. The regional office had incorporated as the Interlake Métis Association Inc. (IMAI), with Gaudry as president. Kingo operated out of a large warehouse-style building in St. Laurent which also served as the office for IMAI. The two companies have a vague sort of rental agreement that traded building improvements paid for by Kingo as credit against unspecified rent payable some time in the future. It's confusing for anyone trying to sort out who owns what, since according to IMAI records, it owns the land and building, but according to land titles and tax roll records, Kingo holds the title.

The financial statements don't help clarify the land status either. The 1991 Kingo statement says

Kingo Fish Products is occupying part of the building owned by Interlake Métis Association., (IMAI) in St. Laurent, Manitoba. In order to occupy this building, Kingo Fish Products had to directly pay for the renovations. It was agreed that the costs which were directly attributed to the building's value would be recorded as a long-term receivable from IMAI. This receivable has no fixed repayment terms and no interest was charged...[10]

The financial records of IMAI also declared the land and building as an asset of the IMAI, recorded before depreciation at $136,527. The statements also acknowledged that the improvements being done to the building by Kingo were to be credited to Kingo against future unspecified rental fees.

But Kingo is the registered owner of the building. According to documents provided by Manitoba Land Titles, Kingo (2381579 Manitoba Ltd.) was registered as title holder of that piece of land on June 22, 1990. The previous registered title holder before that was also Kingo.

Accountant Marcel Blais prepared the financial statements for Kingo up until it was taken over by MMCII. He says it was generally understood that the land and building was purchased on behalf of IMAI, and it was supposed to be transferred after IMAI was incorporated. Blais says there was a change in MMF regional vice-presidents before the incorporation of IMAI, and the original plans were never carried out.

The land in question is smack in the middle of St. Laurent. The building used to be a ladder factory in the days of the Louis Riel Co-op. The co-op was set up by the Métis local in the early 1970s, and the board was chaired by Willie Dumont. For a few years, St. Laurent had a thriving business sector courtesy of economic development grants from the Manitoba government, which also supplied the funding to buy the property and the building on it. More money was used for a 1,700 square foot addition. But, as with most government-funded projects, when the money stopped coming, the co-op folded. The property eventually ended up in the hands of the Royal Bank.

2381576 Manitoba Ltd. (Kingo) later bought the land and buildings, and in 1990, IMAI received a government grant to buy them from Kingo. IMAI's statements for both 1992 and 1993 say: "A grant had been received during the 1990 fiscal year from the Province of Manitoba (Community Places Program) for the purchase of the land and building used by Interlake Métis Association Inc. as a regional office."[11]

However, title remained in the hands of Kingo. To further complicate matters, MMCII included Kingo in its financial records after it took over the company. MMCII's records do not acknowledge Kingo's ownership of about a quarter of the land in downtown St. Laurent or a building valued at over $126,500. MMCII wrote down the value of both its money losers (its construction company and Kingo) giving each a value on the books of one dollar.

LAND TRUSTS

Just to add another wrinkle to who owns what, IMAI is the registered owner of land that is not included in its assets. The IMAI financial statements acknowledge the ownership of about 165 acres of land in St. Laurent, including the land bought just before Joe Clark's visit in the summer of 1991. This land, according to the IMAI records, is being held in trust for the St. Laurent MMF local, and the local is responsible for making the monthly payments on the $44,500 mortgage.

In January of 1992, local MLA Harry Enns presented the IMAI with a cheque from the province for $44,490. The money from Manitoba Community Places was to "help pay for work begun last summer, and for further development of the 160 acres of land stretching from the main road through the village, westward towards Lake Manitoba. A new road was built into the grounds last summer to accommodate the 1991 assembly of the Manitoba Métis and the St. Laurent Métis Days."[12] The grant is not recorded in IMAI's 1992 financial statements. In fact, no information is supplied about the balance owed on the land mortgage or what portion of the debt has been paid off. The statements simply say, "Due to the nature of these funds received, no confirmation as to the balance or obligations in respect of these receipts has been undertaken…." MMCII directors also chose not to include details of its subsidiary holdings in its financial records.

> The financial statements are not prepared on a consolidated basis with those of the Métis Housing Construction Corporation and Kingo Fish Ltd. which are wholly-owned subsidiaries. [They] have not been consolidated because the directors have access to all pertinent information concerning the resources and results of operations of the subsidiaries and have unanimously consented not to have consolidated statements prepared.[13]

It's probably a good thing that Robert Gaudry is a director of the MMF, MMCII, 2381576 Manitoba Ltd. (Kingo), and IMAI. Someone has to be able to keep track of what's going on, when once again, the lines between companies have become blurred.

Kingo has been a puzzle to MMF members for years. Bits and pieces of information leaked out of the MMF head office, often in the way of covertly photocopied documents. Enough people knew enough about money being transferred to Kingo to wonder what was going on. And because of the secrecy around its operations (and those of MMCII), people were suspicious. Even Ernie Blais was refused access to MMCII records when he was president. "MMCII would not let me get into the books, and I'll tell you there were some strange goings-on there...and in the Interlake, Kingo. That's a whole new bag of worms."[14]

The federal and provincial governments continue to fund these companies, despite continued losses. In 1992, MMCII wrote down $131,022 in losses on its subsidiaries. In 1993 and 1994, the MMF records show the head office advanced MMCII, Manitoba Métis Housing Development Inc., Pemmican Publications and Louis Riel Institute more than $800,000. The MMF wrote off 90 percent of that amount as uncollectable. When asked about the continued heavy losses incurred by their business ventures, MMF directors point the finger at the governments who supply them with the money they're losing. Bureaucrats, they say, don't want Métis businesses to succeed, so they don't give the MMF enough money to do a proper job.

Few MMF members could figure out where the money goes and how the companies operate, and MMF financial statements provided to members at annual assemblies didn't include many of the subsidiary companies. These businesses are the domain of a handful of MMF insiders and no one else. The membership has no vested interest in what the MMF does with all the money it gets, so there is no pressure on the MMF or its subsidiaries to tighten up their business practices or to be accountable for where the government funding goes.

SLOPPY PAPERWORK

The auditors reviewing MMF books were not impressed with the organization's business practices.

Corporations run by the MMF would often be dissolved by the Corporations Branch of Manitoba for not filing returns. Manitoba Métis Housing Development Inc. was dissolved in 1987. It was created as a house construction company, but remained inactive until MMCII acquired government funding. It was resurrected in 1990 and the name changed to the Métis Housing Construction Corporation. It promptly lost $192,000.

The Fish Canada Corporation was created to take advantage of the rough fish sales from Kingo. With no business coming from Kingo, the corporate status lapsed in 1994.

If Pemmican Publications were an ordinary business, it would have been in serious trouble in 1989. The publishing company has been one of the MMF's brighter lights since it was created as the Manitoba Métis Federation Press in 1981. It has always had to struggle to find money for publishing, relying on grants from The Canada Council, the Manitoba Arts Council, Manitoba Culture, Heritage and Citizenship, the Association for the Export of Canadian Books and the federal Communications Branch.

Although most of its publications were not expected to become national best sellers, *In Search of April Raintree* did more than that. Pemmican even sold the foreign rights in Europe. However, Pemmican Publications ceased to exist as a legal corporate entity in 1989, simply because no one bothered to keep up the annual returns to the Corporations Branch. In the real business world, this would have been disastrous. With the dissolution of the corporation, the directors would have no legal authority to enter into legal contracts or other agreements. Banks would call in their loans, or move in quickly to protect their collateral.

But MMF businesses didn't operate in the real business world. They rarely did any business with banks, and then only to finance the purchase of land or buildings. The MMF did all its "banking" at the treasuries of the federal and provincial governments. Since funding for the MMF and its assorted subsidiaries has always been political, the MMF's "bankers" were not inclined to jump all over the organization for its sloppy business practices unless it was politically useful to do so.

Other MMF corporations always had their paperwork up to date. The Louis Riel Institute Inc., for instance, was incorporated in 1988 as a Métis education institution. For years, Dumont had been lobbying the province to set up the Louis Riel Institute to do research into Métis history and culture, pull together a library and resource centre on Métis people, and research funding for bursary programs. The MMF wanted base funding of nearly $400,000 a year, with a guarantee of funding for 20 years. It would, of course, be indexed to inflation.

Although Métis leaders, including Dumont, have stated repeatedly that education is the number one priority in helping Métis people, the MMF was not providing any help to Métis students. A former staffer says she would field calls from young people looking for some assistance from the MMF to help them start or continue in university in Winnipeg or Brandon. She had to explain that the MMF didn't have a budget for education.

Some locals, like the one in Churchill, did provide financial support out of money they raised holding bingos and selling break-open tickets. (None of the MMFs local received any financial support from the MMF, except in the form of modest loans that were expected to be repaid.) The Churchill local gave students moving to Winnipeg to go to school a $100 a month subsidy. It wasn't much, but it was more than the MMF was doing.

The MMF does, however, have an education branch, but the branch is one person whose time is largely spent on researching Michif languages and the origins of the Métis.

The paperwork for corporations like MMCII and the Louis Riel Capital Corporation was well looked after. They were vehicles for big time government money.

It was a lot of responsibilty. Yvon Dumont was wearing a dozen different hats. He was president of the MMF, co-chair of the housing committee, ex-officio on every other committee, chairman of Pemmican Publications, president of The Fish Canada Corporation, president of the Louis Riel Institute, and a director of 2381576 Manitoba Ltd. (Kingo), MMCII, and the Métis Housing Construction Corporation.

CHAPTER SEVEN

JUST SAY YES

Indian women were becoming a problem for Yvon Dumont, but more importantly, they were becoming a problem for Brian Mulroney. The Indian women's groups were making noisy objections to the Charlottetown Accord, and they were undermining the credibility of the groups that claimed to speak for them. They were telling the media that the male-dominated organizations like the Assembly of First Nations and the Métis National Council were developing constitutional positions threatening the rights of native women.

Women's issues no longer attracted the general public support they once had, but aboriginal women's issues were starting to catch on. Aboriginal women's groups had been pretty much sidelined in the whole Charlottetown debate, but they were making enough noise to be heard. Aboriginal women had the power to undermine the Yes side's insistence that the Accord was good for native people.

It was Dumont's job to take care of the problem. So, on top of juggling assorted board positions, trying to keep the MMF directors under control, and dealing with the other provincial Métis presidents who were jealous of his close association with the Prime Minister, he now had woman troubles on his hands.

Louise Newans was nearing the end of her term as a report-writer for the Métis senate. The Métis elders had finished up public hearings in Manitoba on the Charlottetown deal. They'd put in some time in Ottawa backing up Dumont, but their job was pretty well done.

Dumont seconded Newans to set up a national Métis women's

organization. The only stipulation was that each of the provincial organizations represented in the national group had to be approved by the provincial Métis association, which meant they also had to support the Charlottetown Accord. There was no room for nay-sayers in the Métis camp.

Métis women had been represented at the MMF board table for years, but the women's group was largely inactive. They weren't getting any money. That changed in 1991 with the creation of the Métis Women of Manitoba (WMOM). Dumont appointed Grace Appleyard as president, but it wasn't until the Métis National Council got its constitutional funding that MWOM got any money. The MNC covered the expenses for the provincial women's group for two years, then after the constitutional money was gone, the MMF started picking up the tab.

Newans and Appleyard met with the Alberta Métis Women's Association in October, 1991. The meeting was a fiasco. Another Métis women's group was claiming the right to speak for Alberta, the National Métis Women of Canada. It was headed by Mary Wiegers, a woman with a mind of her own. Wieger's group stormed the meeting. Newans, as the person organizing the national body, took over as chair. "As chair," she says, "I basically played the ass and did stupid things. [Mary's group] ended up getting more and more angry, and they were already furious. I ended up walking out, and when the chair walks out, there's no more meeting. I did it deliberately."[1]

Wieger's organization did not have the support of the Métis Nation of Alberta or its president, Larry Desmeules. "We later found out that Larry Desmeules was pressured by Yvon to have a women's group that would fall in line with the Alberta Métis Nation. The group there was headed by Mary Wiegers, and Mary was not one to fall in line with Larry. He put a group together and named Sheila Genaille as president."

Not only did Wiegers not support the Métis National Council, she supported the position of the Native Women's Association of Canada that the mainstream native organizations did not represent the interests of Indian and Métis women. But Grace Appleyard knew the right things to say. She presented "The Métis Women's Perspective on National Unity and Constitutional Reform" to the parliamentary committee holding national hearings. It stated "The Métis women of Manitoba represent the concerns of the historical Métis people. We speak in a unified voice with the men of the Métis Nation…."

MWOM was only a month old when it formulated its position supporting whatever the MNC supported. It didn't need to hold lengthy consultations to know what the Métis women of Manitoba were thinking.

Not all native women were as accommodating. The Native Women's Association of Canada went to court in the spring of 1992, asking the Federal Court of Canada to prohibit federal funding for the Métis National Council, the Assembly of First Nations, the Inuit Taparisat of Canada and the Native Council of Canada. The women's group claimed the federal government was violating the equality rights of women and their guarantee of free speech by giving "lavish resources" to the four "male-dominated" aboriginal organizations. NWAC argued it was unfair that those groups were getting $10 million from Ottawa to work on the constitution, while NWAC was getting only $560,000.

Federal Court Judge Allison Walsh wasn't very sympathetic. He said the courts had no authority to tell the federal government how to spend his money. Reporter Joan Bryden covered the daylong hearing, and filed this report on the testy debate between Walsh and the Association's lawyer, Mary Eberts, "...he questioned Eberts' assertion that it's unfair that a group representing 52 percent of the native population gets only five percent of federal funding and no voice at the constitutional table. 'Who gives you the right to speak for all aboriginal women,' he asked. 'Who gives them the right to speak for us,' Eberts shot back."[2]

If Mary Wiegers had any hope of getting on the national Métis women's board, it ended with a letter she sent to NWAC offering moral support for the court case.

> Traditionally, Métis National Council has opposed the advance-ment of equality rights for women. In fact, MNC refuses to recognize the National Métis Women of Canada.... National Métis Women of Canada require equal representation to that of the Métis National Council in terms of both funding which is intended to deal with constitutional matters as well as equal representation at the constitutional table for the Canada Round discussion.[3]

Such insurgent voices needed to be drowned out. Dumont wanted the Métis women's group up and running. Within two weeks of the court case, the provincial Métis women's groups met in Winnipeg. Wiegers was not invited. The group unanimously approved the creation of a national group, and in June, the Métis National Council of Women Inc. (MNCW) became the official voice of Métis women. The freshly-minted Métis women's group joined the Yes campaign team with great enthusiasm. As the date for the Charlottetown referendum drew closer, the MNCW dismissed the concerns raised by other native women's groups that women were not being heard in the constitutional process.

President Sheila Genaille said Métis women weren't at all concerned about the issue of gender equality in the Charlottetown Accord. "As full partners in the Métis Nation, and having participated fully in shaping the Métis constitutional strategy, Métis women are proud of the gains we have achieved under the Canada Round." In fact, said Genaille, Métis culture "was unlikely to produce gender discrimination." The MNCW stated: "Failure to ratify this agreement will bring all members of the Métis Nation back to square one. That is why Métis women will campaign alongside Métis men, for the "Yes" side of the referendum."[4]

Newans says she thought setting up the national Métis women's group was the right thing to do. She figured it had a lot of potential. She's not so sure now. Newans says she now realizes it was created only to provide an aboriginal women's group that would support the Prime Minister, and cancel out the aboriginal women's voices that opposed him. As national Métis leader, Dumont needed to appear to speak for both Métis men and women. "It was all done to make Yvon look good," says Newans.

But the battle to keep Métis women firmly on the Yes side reared up again in the last critical weeks before the referendum. Grace Appleyard had been replaced as president of the Métis Women of Manitoba by Sandra Delaronde, a cousin of Billyjo's. Delaronde had been involved in Métis politics for several years, but was a fringe player. She didn't support the National Métis Council of Women's viewpoint on Charlottetown, and said so. It brought an immediate response from Sheila Genaille, who expressed her shock and amazement that the Métis women in Manitoba would speak against the national body. "I was also totally surprised that the Métis Women of Manitoba would take a No stand at this late date, because if the Charlottetown Agreement is not ratified, the Métis Nation will be back to square one."[5]

Sandra was quickly shushed, and made to see the error of her ways. She could have her own opinion on Charlottetown, but she was expected to keep it to herself. The MMF had little room for people who didn't play the game.

CHAPTER EIGHT

A POISON PILL

Elections in the MMF have routinely been accompanied by stories of fraud, coercion, intimidation and vote-buying. It sometimes got ugly in the political arena, but it was never uglier or sleazier than after the departure of Yvon Dumont.

The day before the whole MMF board and senior staff members flew to Vancouver for Dumont's final board meeting, he authorized a number of payments, including $3,000 for Delaronde for "expenses incurred in the investigation of the disappearance of the Bell of Batoche from the legion in Millbrook, Ontario."[1] Dumont told staff that Delaronde didn't have to make an accounting of his "investigation" to anyone.

The bell was first taken as a war trophy from the church in Batoche in 1885 following the battle that put an end to the Northwest Rebellion. The soldier who took the bell was from Ontario, and it ended up in the Royal Canadian Legion hall in Millbrook. Dumont and Delaronde both visited the Legion in the fall of 1991. A week after their visit, the bell was stolen.

Delaronde was widely rumoured to have information on the location of the missing bell, but when asked if he knew where it was, he would just smile and say "No comment." The bell has never resurfaced. The police don't appear to be hot on the trail either. Officials with both the Winnipeg Police Service and the RCMP appear to be under the impression the other is in charge of investigating the theft.

Before Dumont left office, he authorized a $3,000 advance for Delaronde along with a big chunk of holiday pay. The personnel administrator was having a hard time figuring out Delaronde's holiday pay since he wouldn't follow office policy. "Because Billyjo does not keep time sheets," she wrote in a memo to Dumont, "or fill out the necessary vacation requests and objected to the receptionist tracking his time, there is no possible way for me to establish the number of holidays taken."[2] Dumont authorized holiday pay for nine weeks, and informed the personnel administrator via memo that Billyjo's position was special, and he didn't need to adhere to MMF policy.

There wasn't a flurry of special appointments to committees and company boards that often accompany a change in leadership. The insiders were expecting to retain control of the MMF and its operations once Dumont left. No one imagined that Ernie Blais was about to snatch away the king's crown. As a director and co-chair of the housing committee, Blais was close enough to the insiders to be suspicious about their activities. But because so much of the MMF business was secret, he didn't really know what was going on. It would be easy enough to keep him in the dark until he could be gotten rid of in the up-coming election.

The insiders weren't really afraid of Blais, but they were afraid of John Morrisseau. Morrisseau was just back from a stint working with the Royal Commission on Aboriginal Peoples. After his surprise election in Vancouver as the interim president, Blais cleaned house. When Blais fired Ed Swain and hired Morrisseau as the new general manager, the insiders started getting nervous. Morrisseau was not only a long-time foe of the Dumont camp, he knew from past experience how the MMF operated and how the game was played. He was far more dangerous to the status quo than Blais.

Blais changed the locks on the MMF offices and fired a number of staff members who were not predisposed to cooperating with the new regime. "I don't enjoy laying people off," said Blais. "I think it's a sad day when I have to do it, but things are necessary."[3] "It's disgusting," huffed Sandra Delaronde, the president of the Métis Women of Manitoba. "If we can't protect the rights of single parents and young women within our own organization, how can we protect the rights of people in our nation?"[4]

The new interim president was facing a financial mess. The MMF was $400,000 in the red, and Blais had an uncooperative board on his hands. He didn't make it any easier on himself when he ordered a stop to all the committee meetings. The directors didn't like that one bit. "We're spending money needlessly on committees." said Blais. "It's committees, committees, committees…and they only want more committees so they can have more money in their pockets. When you get $200 per meeting, they want it more and more."[5]

A manager who was working in the head office says she was appalled by the amount of cash she saw leaving the building. "[The directors] go wild when they have committee meetings. They would go to three committee meetings a day and walk out with huge sums of money. They'll go to Housing for an hour or so, go to Tripartite and it's the same thing. They focused on the three main programs that have money—Child and Family, Tripartite and Housing. They'd get a lot of money." She was worried all the committee meetings were bleeding the MMF dry. But it didn't really matter. Everyone was too busy plotting election strategy to worry much about the day-to-day operations of the MMF. Any pretense of cooperation disappeared when the board hired Dumont's former personnel manager, Laura Guiboche, as the chief electoral officer. Blais' people had wanted one of their own people in the job.

Laura Guiboche said she moved the election staff out of head office and into the MMCII-owned building to avoid political interference. She was working out of the back of an unfinished office without proper flooring, but she did have a couple of battered old desks, a couple of phones and an answering machine. That's when the death threats started. Guiboche said the two messages left on the answering machine threatened the lives of her and her family. Police investigated, but no charges were laid. It set the tone for the campaign. There was a lot at stake for the old Dumont camp. They faced losing all the hard work they'd put into building up their regional offices if Blais was re-elected. Someone else would be collecting the spoils of power.

But Blais wasn't afraid of death threats. He said it helped that his cousin Larry Hallet was president of the Los Bravos biker gang, although that didn't stop people from occasionally making nasty calls. "You get those things. I just shrug it off. I think people are afraid of me because of my association with Larry. I think that's the major thing. That's why people don't bother me."[6]

The public squabbling was getting uglier, with each faction accusing the other of attempting to hijack the election process. "We're our own worst enemies," said Louise Perry, a regional director from The Pas. "It's not anybody out there, it's us ourselves and what we do to each other. There are a lot of Métis people out there who will have absolutely nothing to do with the MMF because they see it as an organization that can't get along and aren't willing to work together to solve problems and look at the real issues."[7] Blais was promising a new order at the MMF, with more grassroots involvement—giving the MMF back to the people. It touched a chord with MMF members. In a record turn-out for the October election, Blais was returned to power. Despite Delaronde's best efforts to draw on the support he used to deliver for Dumont, he was firmly in second place. Delaronde might have been able to take the race if Ed Swain, also from the Dumont camp, hadn't split the vote by deciding to run for president, too.

OUSTING THE PRESIDENT

The old guard wasn't beaten. A month after the election, the newly elected board met for the first time in Winnipeg the night before the beginning of the 1993 annual assembly. Just minutes into the November 12 meeting, David Chartrand (Elbert's brother) made a motion to remove the President. It was seconded by Denise Thomas, another of the insiders. Blais, they said, was a tyrant and dictator, proved by his cancelling committee meetings. The motion passed, 13-9. The board then appointed Bill Flamand as general manager, since it was just as important to get rid of Morrisseau as it was to get Blais out of the way.

That night the insiders had the locks changed on the MMF offices, and put a security guard on the door. Ernie Blais was officially locked out. The assembly descended into disarray the next morning as word spread about the president being forced out. It was, said some, just a continuation of the election battle.

Bill Flamand was chairing the meeting, but allowed Blais to speak when he asked to address the assembly. Blais offered to resign, but only if the board members would resign as well. Until then, he considered himself still president of the MMF. Blais promptly got a temporary court injunction ordering the dissident board members to turn the MMF's keys over, and confirm his position as president. Blais showed up at the MMF office accompanied by city police officers and a clutch of reporters and television cameras, and made a grand re-entry.

The dissidents requested that the court rescind the order, and if not, to appoint a receiver to run the MMF. Anything but Ernie. The whole issue was back in court a few days later.

This time Judge Monnin had strong words for the warring parties.

I gave strong consideration to appointing the receiver the defendants requested. I finally decided not to because I believe, strange
as it may seem, that such an appointment might well precipitate the
total disintegration of the MMF. The organization is in the throes
of a crisis. If that crisis is not dealt with in a democratic fashion by
men and women of goodwill, the whole *raison d'etre* of the
organization will cease to exist.[8]

Perhaps if Judge Monnin had been more familiar with Métis politics,
he would have realized that a generosity of spirit and a willingness to
compromise were nowhere in evidence. There has never been a middle
ground in MMF politics.

Monnin ordered Blais to get the board together for a meeting within
two weeks. He advised them to either sort it out, or have the integrity to
make use of the proper provisions set out in the MMF constitution for
dissolving the board and calling a new election.

On December 8, 1993, the board met in The Pas. Again David
Chartrand made a motion requesting Blais resign. Again, Denise Thomas
seconded it. Blais challenged the dissidents to explain what they were
doing. "I asked them, 'On what basis are you removing me,' and David
Chartrand's exact words were 'Oh, a bunch of reasons.' I asked him what
specifically because we might be going to court on this. [He said], 'Any
reason. You pick any reason you want.' So that was it."

Blais agreed to resign under the constitutional clause that requires all
board members to resign as well. Everyone but the newly-elected president
of the Métis Women of Manitoba voted in favour of the motion. "The
reason my supporters voted in favour," said Blais, "is because they didn't
want to see me being put through this kind of abuse anymore, so they said,
'this is the best way out.'"

The entire board had resigned. The MMF was in limbo. Morrisseau,
who had returned as general manager when Blais was allowed back into the
MMF offices, knew something had to be done. The organization needed a
board of directors to hold an election to elect a new board of directors. He
asked the court to appoint an interim board. A group of the old guard
vehemently opposed the court application. It appears the last thing they
wanted was outsiders moving in. But on December 20, 1993, Madame
Justice Ruth Krindle delivered the poison pill. She appointed the requested

interim board. The MMF was no longer under the control of the Métis, nor was it under the control of the government.

And who were the new directors of the MMF? The Honourable Ed Schreyer, the former Governor General of Canada; Lesia Szwaluk, executive director of the North Winnipeg YW/YMCA; and Menno Wiebe from the Mennonite Central Committee. The new directors were people of impeccable credentials, albeit with political leanings somewhat to the left. The three, said Krindle, were stepping into the fray at a time of crisis.

It is clear they did so out of a sense of public duty and out of a desire to assist the Métis people in Manitoba at a time when their governing organization was in crisis. Without the assistance of those and other like-minded people, the organization would simply have been incapable of functioning. The regional corporations were legally unable to step into the breach to administer the on-going programs because they too were without directors. The appointment of these three individuals to act as interim directors of the MMF was acceptable to all the defendants. No aboriginal person was able to be agreed upon by them.[9]

As a final indignity to the insiders, the interim board kept Morrisseau on as general manager. "We didn't know the history (of the MMF)," says Szwaluk. "We didn't know the historical factors…how elections were done in the past, and what were some of the downfalls of the last election. We needed information. Is this really part of a holding company? Is this not? John had that at his fingertips."[10] Szwaluk says Morrisseau was perceived as a Blais supporter, and many of the former directors thought he would give biased advice to the interim board. They deluged Szwaluk with phone calls and faxes making allegations about a dark past. "There was tons of stuff…tacky, stupid stuff. I said, 'prove it to me. Where's the evidence?'" She says Morrisseau was as unbiased as anybody could be in that position, and there simply wasn't a person on the face of the earth who wouldn't have been accused of political bias by one side or the other.

Most of the workload fell of Szwaluk's shoulders. She was responsible for authorizing expenditures, and since she lived near the MMF head office, she was most accessible. Szwaluk requested that all outstanding invoices from the regional offices be forwarded to her for payment. She quickly discovered that the regional vice-presidents were under the illusion that it was business as usual in their little empires. They wanted their usual quarterly transfer payments from head office.

"They thought they could continue operating each region separately," says Blais, "and still be within their own little domain and they wouldn't be affected [by the interim board]. So the vice-president of the South-east region and the vice-president of the Interlake region continued with their own thing, with their own board of directors. That's how it was set up."[11] The vice-presidents howled in protest at having to be answerable to the interim board, or they hired lawyers to howl for them. The board said it would allow the locals of each region to select a manager to run the region's on-going programs, but the money was going to stay under the control of the court-appointed board.

Szwaluk says it was apparent early on that there were problems with how the regions were handling their money. "They were using other money to cover expenses between transfer payments, and then of course, when transfer payment didn't come in December, a lot of regions were caught in the lurch."[12] Szwaluk says that's when the interim board decided they'd better protect themselves by bringing in an auditing firm. They didn't want to be later accused of being responsible for the financial mismanagement they suspected was going on. The interim board wanted to be very clear about what had happened to the money prior to their appointment, and what they did with the money for as long as they were in charge of the MMF. They realized they'd better hire their own lawyer, too, and keep him close at hand.

But the Interlake, Winnipeg, The Pas and South-east vice-presidents were already trying to by-pass the board by going directly to the government. Ottawa had continued sending cheques to the MMF after the interim board took over, but the provincial funding had stopped. The vice-presidents were lobbying Northern Affairs Minister Darren Praznik to by-pass the MMF head office and give them the money. In an activity report from January, 1994, director Louise Perry from The Pas wrote, "Met with the Minister of Northern Affairs regarding transfer payments to this office. Our situation is becoming grave in terms of paying our obligations to our creditors and payroll for the Core Staff. In our meeting with the Minister we made it clear that the role of the Interim Board of the MMF should in no way affect the continuing operations of this regional office, and that they have used Métis politics to interfere."

Some dissident directors began a lobbying campaign to convince the funders of MMF programs that the interim board was not to be trusted, and funding was to be sent to the regional offices instead. Then they started what amounted to a harassment campaign against Szwaluk. She says she was never threatened the way some other people were, but the constant badgering and harassment were worse. "There'd be phone calls at midnight, and calls at five in the morning. People saying 'don't do it' and then hanging up. People coming to see me. It was like the more you bug her, maybe she'll finally break down. I wasn't afraid...the whole thing just pissed me off." Szwaluk was the target of most of the harassment because she was an easier target, but Schreyer and Wiebe got calls, too. "They had a weird telephone campaign going. They would phone and say weird things [like] 'why are we paying these bills? And why are we paying this bill?' How did they know what we were doing? Who was the spy? It was like we made a decision and then all of a sudden everyone knew...and then the phone calls would start."[13]

Szwaluk says the level of distrust within the organization was very disturbing. "That distrust was such a hateful distrust. That to me was so shocking. I've worked in a lot of organizations, and I've never seen that kind of hatred. And doing things to hurt each other. It was very much a power struggle."

Most of the regional directors (Thompson, Dauphin and South-west directors being the exceptions) were refusing to forward bills for payment, refusing to be in any way answerable to Morrisseau, and refusing to cooperate with requests for information from Deloitte & Touche, the interim board's auditor.

The dissident directors began court action to stop the interim board from hiring regional managers. Szwaluk had had enough. She went back to Judge Krindle on March 7, 1994 to get the interim board's jurisdiction settled. "It has become evident that there is no common ground between the various factions within the MMF," she told Krindle. "Consequently, it has been impossible for the interim board by consensus to administer the business and financial affairs of the MMF." Krindle ruled that since the regional corporations were without directors or officers, the interim board had a duty to not transfer funds or leave program administration to corporations that were not legally functioning. She gave the interim board the endorsement they needed. Krindle also approved the extension of the audit to include not only the head office and the housing branch, but the regional offices as well. Szwaluk says once the dissidents realized the interim board had the weight of the courts behind them, they backed off. But they didn't become any more cooperative.

CRACKING THE REGIONAL OFFICES

The interim board stood firm on having invoices forwarded to head office for payment. The regions initially refused to submit the necessary paperwork, and then only when services like telephones and electricity were about to be cut off. The Dauphin regional office, for instance, had run up an $8,000 phone bill and was about to be disconnected. Even though the transfer payments received until the interim board took over had a generous allotment for phones, no payments had been made to Manitoba Telephone System since March, 1993.

In the Interlake office, the auditors scratched their heads over the incestuous relationships between the Interlake Métis Association, Kingo, and St. Laurent Wood Products, which was under the name of Canada Leaf Cutter Bee (1987) Limited. According to the auditor's report, St. Laurent Wood Products was covering the salaries of the regional staff and paid IMAI's $2,579 hydro bill. The regional office was scrambling without funding coming from the MMF head office. The property taxes owed to the RM of St. Laurent were heavily in arrears, and so were the employee deductions payable to Revenue Canada.

The Pas regional office had not been paying its mortgage and taxes either. The money allocated to cover those expenses in the transfer payments had gone somewhere else.

Louise Perry, the MMf director from The Pas regional office who had earlier said MMF members had to work together to solve their differences, refused to cooperate in any way with the interim board. She dared them to fire her. They did.

According to the interim's board final report to the court, Perry and Sandra Delaronde had continued signing legal contracts, even though they were told they had no authority to do so. They also continued writing cheques. About 150 cheques were covered with the government funding that was supposed to be used to run employment programs. The report states, "It appears that monies received through programs were used to pay wages and expenses directly from the Regional Corporation rather than submitted to the MMF for payment as directed by the Interim Board. Monies received from bingos (through the Lotteries Commission) have been used for these purposes rather than those purposed set out in its license."

All the regions eventually cracked, and started sending in invoices for payment. The directors knew many of the invoices they were sending in were supposed to have been already paid, and that continually raised the question about where that money had gone.

The Winnipeg regional office held out the longest, but it did it by jeopardizing the graduation of 15 Métis students. Employment and Immigration Canada was paying for the students to attend Red River Community College (RRCC) in Winnipeg through a program called Pathways. The government program had been set up to be run by the Winnipeg regional office.

David Chartrand and the other Winnipeg directors opted to keep the regional office running and pay staff, instead of paying the students' tuition. Szwaluk says the interim board had no choice but to bail the students out. "When we took over, RRCC threatened that they would not graduate the fifteen students because they had not been paid.... It was unfair that because of what happened in the region they would not graduate." The interim board paid $42,000 to the college, and later received another invoice for an additional $28,000.

Szwaluk says the directors were using the training money to cover their expenses, counting on the Northern Affairs minister turning the provincial funding over to them. "They thought that by getting to the Minister that they were going to get the money directly to themselves, but it didn't work." The interim board needed the provincial funding, as well. They were just as short of cash. Szwaluk met several times with Darren Praznik, and found it frustrating that he continued to hold the money back. He was refusing to release the $140,000 balance of the province's contribution to Tripartite, and $98,300 of core funding. "That sort of disheartened us, because we were court appointed. We've got to pay the damned bills and we're not getting the money. That made me very irritable, and I said to him, 'Look, we cannot do the job without the money. You've always dished it out. Why all of a sudden now you're not? Because there are faxes coming from your region. Because they're coming from your constituents? Well, too bad.'"

The provincial Tories had been generally supportive of the MMF operations with all its flaws and questionable operations since the early Dumont years. Praznik had a particular interest in not upsetting South-east vice-president Denise Thomas. Her region encompassed his constituency, and she was making her wishes known, loud and clear. Praznik told the interim board he wasn't releasing the money because of suspected irregularities by the interim board. "I regret to advise that serious concerns have been raised with me and my Department by various members of the Manitoba Métis Federations' regional organizations which suggest irregularities in the disbursements of regional grants and the applications of monies disbursed, as well as withholding of funds designated for certain regions."[14]

The dissidents were telling Praznik that Morrisseau was paying out program money only to the regions that had supported Ernie Blais in the last election, and punishing the other regions because of politics. Their hatred of Morrisseau was clear, and they believed the interim board was in cahoots with him, or, at the very least, being manipulated by him. They ignored the fact that the regions which were getting money had cooperated with the board and the auditors, and the interim board was assured the money was going where it was supposed to. Praznik chose to side with the dissidents.

RED FLAGS

The two accounting firms hired by the interim board to audit the MMF head office, the housing branch and the regional corporations were having a tough time. They were being paid to audit and prepare financial statements for the MMF fiscal year ending March 31, 1994. But it was hard going with some of the regional offices resisting all the way. In the end, the accountants' analysis of the regional office was given in the form of a denial of opinion. Without access to certain documents, they couldn't verify the accuracy of the financial statements they were preparing. The only region to get the accountants' stamp of approval was the Southwest (Brandon) region. The Pas, Thompson, Dauphin, Winnipeg, South-east, and Interlake regions all had irregularities in their financial records.

Deloitte & Touche prepared a lengthy document for the interim board, detailing the many problem areas they'd discovered and recommending actions that a new MMF board could take to clear up the trouble spots. Those recommendations included making the regional offices accountable to head office for how they were spending the money transferred to them, and cleaning up sloppy business practices in both the regions and the head office.

In recent months, funders have become increasingly pressed to trim their budgets. As they make future funding decisions, they will likely assess each of the grants they currently make to determine the social benefit created by each. They will also likely increase the control and accountability requirements associated with their provision of funding. In this environment, confidence of the funders in the organizations they provide grants to is paramount.[15]

The Winnipeg region's handling of Pathways funds that were supposed to pay for the Red River College students, noted the accountants, was an example of how the MMF was jeopardizing future Pathways programs. Other Pathways programs were being administered in some regions under separate corporations so that the program funding was not accounted for in the regional statements. This hurt, because the MMF under Dumont had been lobbying hard to have the millions of federal dollars going to Pathways aboriginal employment and training programs split between the Indians and Métis with, of course, the MMF in total control of the money designated for the Métis.

The accountants noticed the extensive losses the MMF head office had incurred by giving out uncollectable personal loans, and advised the MMF to stop making personal loans altogether. Head office loans to assorted subsidiaries were also questioned. The auditors noted the MMF was writing off heavy losses from its subsidiaries and there was little accountability to the MMF for the use of the loans. The auditors did not have the authority to investigate the subsidiaries, other than the regional corporations, but they red-flagged the subsidiaries as a serious problem area for the proper management of the MMF.

The auditors were waving lots of red flags over the MMF's handling of cash. They noted that the same person taking in cash was also giving it out without it being monitored by a second person. Money was being transferred from one corporate bank account to another without explanation, and some transfers were being made to personal accounts as well. The accountants didn't like the large amounts of cash left sitting in an unlocked desk drawer, and disapproved of cash being taken out of the bank to pay the directors' per diems. They warned the MMF that Revenue Canada required honoraria totaling more than $500 year to be claimed as taxable income, and the MMF should have been issuing the appropriate T-4A slips.

The lengthy reports prepared by the auditors detailed more than thirty problems in the way money was being handled in the head office and housing branch. More than sixty problem areas in the regions were pointed out, from missing documents to unexplained payments to staff and directors. The auditors weren't mandated to search for wrongdoing or comment on the appropriateness of transactions. That would have required a forensic audit. Their job was limited to making sure the paperwork was there for the money coming in and the money going out.

ELECTION FEVER

The interim board's mandate was to run the MMF in the absence of elected officials, and organize the election of a new board. The biggest problem the interim board had right off the top was finding a suitable Chief Electoral Officer. It was obvious that no one in Métis political circles would do, since they would be either in the Blais camp or the Delaronde camp. That thankless task was taken on by Alvin Hamilton, a retired Associate Chief Justice of the Manitoba Court of Queen's Bench. Hamilton was respected in the aboriginal community, having co-chaired Manitoba's Aboriginal Justice Inquiry several years before along with judge Murray Sinclair. Hamilton appointed a review panel to help him, including Winnipeg aboriginal activist Sandy Funk and the manager of the Métis housing construction company, Don Roulette. The election was set for June 23, 1994.

There were lots of wrinkles to iron out, not the least of which was deciding who should be allowed to vote in the MMF election. The CEO wanted to avoid scenes from previous elections where intoxicated people from nearby bars were encouraged to vote for a certain candidate, after a friendly drink or two with campaign workers. All they had to do was declare their Métis status at the polling station to be eligible to vote. Judge Krindle settled that issue during the March 7 court hearing. She ruled that only MMF members whose names were on the voter's lists could vote for the new board of directors. To back up its claim to represent all Métis people, the MMF had been letting anyone vote in its elections and at the annual assemblies. Krindle's decision was a reminder that the MMF represented only those people who chose to take out membership cards.

While Hamilton and the courts were sorting out the technicalities of the election, the candidates were pulling out all the stops. The old insiders wanted back in, and that meant using whatever method was necessary to undermine the credibility of Blais supporters.

Christine Lavallee was one of the early casualties. The president of the Métis Women of Manitoba had made her support for Blais very clear at the November annual assembly when the insiders first tried to oust Blais. A whisper campaign started, suggesting Lavallee was involved in some kind of theft. No one knew what it was, but maybe it had something to do with her children. And had anyone heard anything about Lavallee taking the money for the food at last year's cultural reunion? What about poor Christine's mental stability?

One MWOM director later testfied at a court hearing that Deborah Barron-McNabb told her, "...Christine was never allowed to be anywhere by herself because they, and I'm not sure who they were, were afraid of what she might say. [There] always had to be someone from the MMF or her husband with her to monitor what she was saying...she wasn't well mentally, and that's why the people always had to be around her."[16]

At a February meeting that Lavallee did not attend, five of the seven MWOM directors approved a motion to remove Lavallee from office and give Barron-McNabb the presidency. Barron-McNabb called the *Winnipeg Free Press* to let them in on what was happening. Under cross-examination, Barron-McNabb said, "When the press contacted me or when, I'm sorry, when I spoke to the *Winnipeg Free Press*, they asked me [for] what reasons she was removed.... They pressed me for more information and I said I would not elaborate on that because I didn't want to interfere in any investigation that might continue."[17]

There was no investigation. The most significant financial irregularity turned out to be the accusation that Lavallee had opened a bank account at the Me-Dian Credit Union and hid it from the other directors. Under cross-examination, Barron-McNabb admitted the account had been opened to take a deposit from the MMF for MWOM about a month before Lavallee was elected to office, but she rationalized that since Lavallee was the first to use the account, she was somehow retroactively responsible for setting it up and not telling the other directors. "Mr. Morrisey, from the Credit Union, that was his position, that Christine had opened the bank account due to the fact there was no signature on the account and hers was one of the...was the first signature."[18]

Not surprisingly, the court supported Lavallee's bid to get her presidency back.

The sleaze level of the campaign plummeted to a new low with the publication of *Crosshairs!*, a newsletter describing itself as "an information newspaper produced and distributed by the Committee to Save the MMF." No names appeared in the newsletter to claim credit for the publication, but it was clearly coming from the Blais camp. It was full of tasty little snippets naming names, under the heading of

"Do You Know?..."

That our naughty boy - - - is facing disciplinary action from his employer? We hear he called one of the Interim Board members a F-ing B-ch. Way to be a leader - - -.

Anybody remember when - - - was bragging about his bedroom acrobatics with a prominent NDP MLA? Apparently - - - was so impressed, she gave him a plum job in government. We wonder who he's in the bedroom with now?

A little update on the whereabouts of the Bell of Batoche. The bell stolen from a Catholic church in Batoche in Saskatchewan is sacred to the church. We have received information that the bell is in the hands of certain unscrupulous individuals who bring the bell out of hiding when they are in the heat of parties. Drunken revellers get to take turns ringing the bell. It's sad that something that means so much to the Métis people of Saskatchewan is in the hands of some drunken fools who just don't care.

It went on and on in the same vein. The Delaronde camp responded with a *Crosshairs!* edition of its own. Some of the candidates started adding stories of their own and tacking then up in public places in the regions, like this story attacking a woman running for the board:

Why do you think - - - couldn't get along with the female regional staff!!! At best it's hard to work and concentrate when she is looking at you up and down, while licking her lips!! When talking to - - - , and if you're a female, she is always quoted as saying to them, WE FEMALES HAVE TO STICK TOGETHER, Come on, - - -, how close do you want to get? Take your mind out of the gutter once in a while....

Even *Frank* magazine got into the act, thoroughly slamming Blais and John Morrisseau in a review of the "Manitoba Métis Mutiny."

Blais was campaigning on the ticket of saving the Manitoba Métis Federation and making it accountable to the membership. He was proposing to change the one-member, one-vote system to the delegate system that Stan Fulham had set up in the first years of the MMF. That worried people who interpreted it as taking power away from individuals. But Blais' real weakness was representing himself as more honest than other presidential candidates. The Delaronde camp undermined Blais' credibility by accusing him of altering legal documents, shredding incriminating papers and giving jobs to his political allies. Blais, on the other hand, had made use of his time in the head office to dig up documents to "prove" Delaronde was unfit to be president.

Both sides took their "proof" to the media, but most journalists had gotten tired of one side or the other trying to use them. Since it was no longer possible to tell who, if anyone, was telling the truth, the media backed off. No one associated with the MMF had any credibility anymore, and journalists preferred to avoid being sucked into the quagmire of Métis politics.

Just a week before the election, a fax arrived for Szwaluk. On the single sheet was written, "To: Leisa Szwaluk, YMCA. We hope you win Ernie's jacket!!!," referring to a fund-raising raffle on Blais' jacket. At the bottom of the page was a photocopy of an MMF cheque made payable to the Ernie Blais Campaign Fund in the amount of $17,750, with the signatures of Szwaluk and Morrisseau. "I know I didn't sign a cheque for seventeen thousand dollars. And of course, when we started looking at the signature, it wasn't my signature. It was a very good forgery. And John Morrisseau's was a forgery, but I think it was a very good forgery in that I think it was sort of clipped out and traced."[19]

The interim board tried to figure out where the cheque might have come from. It turned out to be a voided cheque from a series used in 1989. "When we looked at the series," says Szwaluk, "that cheque was missing from the series, and on the stub, the word 'void' was written out.... So someone kept that cheque in their pocket for God knows how long. Or it was someone in the office who went through the old files and pulled this cheque out."[20]

The objective was fairly clear. The photocopy was "proof" that the interim board was indeed in league with Blais, and was using MMF funds for his campaign. In one fell swoop, both Blais and the interim board would be discredited. "I was very, very angry," says Szwaluk. "I felt it was a real smear campaign in the elections, and they really tried to prove to other people in the MMF that we were Ernie Blais supporters, which I think was very wrong. [Attacking] the integrity of the three board members, regardless of whose signature was on there, was a real slap in the face. ... We were trying to keep their organization afloat."

Blais screamed bloody murder, accusing Delaronde of trying to frame him. Delaronde denied it. "I, in no way, shape or form had anything to do with the writing of that cheque," Delaronde said.[21] Delaronde said someone had gotten hold of MMF documents in his handwriting so the cheque could be forged to match his penmanship. He suggested the forgery was an attempt to discredit him, by making people think he was responsible for trying to set up Blais.

But the damage was done. The old order was returned to power. All that was left was to minimize the damage the interim board might do, having been the only outsiders to get a close-up look at the bowels of the MMF.

Business as Usual

Yvon Dumont was firmly ensconsed in Government House, and his former second-in-command was the MMF president-elect. The day after the election, Northern Affairs minister Darren Praznik gave the MMF all the provincial funding he'd been holding back. And Delaronde took legal action against the interim board. He was acknowledged as the new president, but he couldn't get into the MMF offices until the election was officially declared. In his affidavits to the court, Delaronde accused the interim board of removing and shredding MMF documents and sought an injunction to prevent further destruction of documents. He wanted the court to declare him president immediately. The action was dismissed by the judge and Delaronde was ordered to pay the costs of the MMF and the interim board.

Judge Ruth Krindle took an unflattering view of Delaronde's allegations.

The allegations conjure up visions of the former Governor General of Canada, the Director of the Mennonite Central committee and the Executive Director of the North End Y all attempting furiously to destroy the records of their own misdeeds. Whether that was the intent of the applicant or not, it is difficult to read the statement of claim without gaining the clear impression that what was being publicly alleged was the complicity of the interim board in a deliberate removal and destruction of MMF property.[22]

Delaronde couldn't become MMF president until the chief electoral officer had satisfied himself that the various election irregularities had not compromised the outcome of the vote. He was officially declared president on July 3. One of the first actions of the new board was to stop payment on all the outstanding cheques written by the interim board. The MMF alleged in court the interim board was running the MMF into the ground and leaving it with a deficit of over $1 million. It also stated, amongst other allegations, that in the two days before the new board took over, Morrisseau had paid out over $300,000 to his friends.

A short time later, the new MMF board filed what Krindle called "the most scandalous affidavits I have ever seen...affidavits which in my opinion impugned the motives, the integrity and the intelligence of the members of the interim board." Following a heated discussion in the courtroom, the three offending affidavits were withdrawn, and a replacement affidavit was filed. By the time the dust had settled, only a few of the interim board's decisions were being questioned. The final act of the interim board, in completing the action that had started when Morrisseau requested a court-appointed board, was to have the handling of the finances approved.

Krindle delivered her judgement on November 4, 1994.

I find that the interim board discharged its responsibilities to a high standard indeed. Their honesty and integrity are above reproach. They have tried, sometimes under impossible circumstances, to remain apart from the political divisions which threaten to destroy the MMF. They undertook the responsibility because of their commitment to the Métis people of Manitoba and it was that commitment alone which permitted them to continue to function in the terrible position in which they found themselves. They were subject to personal attacks, direct and indirect, on their integrity and honesty, none of which had any merit whatsoever. They may not have taken on this responsibility because they expected someone to say 'thank-you' to them, but they are entitled to be thanked, and they should be thanked, by the people who directly benefited from their strength and commitment, the Métis people of Manitoba.[23]

When asked if she'd found anything positive in her time on the interim board, Szwaluk says there wasn't much. "Certainly the chance to work with Ed and Menno. That was number one. And seeing the people who really believed in the organization, even people like John Morrisseau. Regardless of the flak that guy took, he believed in the MMF and he worked in it. He took a lot of shit, and if I was him I would have quit as general manager." Those who had believed they could change the MMF gave up. They had no heart left to fight for change.

Schreyer was not as involved as Szwaluk in the nitty gritty of running the MMF, but he was shocked at how different the organization was from the one he'd known in the early 1970s. "I knew there were problems," he said, "but I had no idea how bad they were."

CHAPTER NINE

BETRAYED

The Manitoba Métis Federation has hurt the very people it purports to represent. The insiders who knew how the game was played wrapped themselves in the Métis flag, pledged allegiance to the Métis nation, and loudly condemned government for oppressing the Métis and forcing them to live in poverty. The government was the enemy and the MMF (and its national body, the Métis National Council) were the defenders of the people. But the MMF and MNC had more often than not been allies of government, so who, then, was really the enemy? It appears the enemy was anyone from the Métis community who would dare to threaten the power of the government sanctioned advocacy group.

L'Union Nationale Métisse Saint-Joseph du Manitoba became the enemy when it dared to contradict the MMF and MNC leaders for claiming to be the only true voice of Métis people. The MMF and MNC leaders claimed total control of government-funded programs, some of which were designated not only for the Métis poor but non-Métis poor as well. They also claimed for themselves the right to control billions of dollars anticipated from land claim settlements, and legislated control of all Métis living on a yet to be acquired land base. Members of L'Union Nationale said it was a more credible representative of the Métis of the Red River Settlement. "L'Union Nationale Métisse St. Joseph du Manitoba," said Louis Riel's grand-niece Augustine Abraham, "continuously in existence since 1887, is the only Métis organization started by the Métis for the Métis and funded by themselves. All others had their beginnings 25 years ago or less through the efforts and funding of government bureaucracies. They continue to live off this funding. The old saying is, 'who pays the piper calls the tune.'"[1]

Minding the Money

Since government was calling the tune, political leaders had the ability to force the MMF and MNC to be accountable by using nothing more than the threat of withholding funding. Government had a moral obligation, as well, to demand accountability because the bundles of money they were giving the MMF and MNC had been taken from the pockets of Canadian taxpayers. With rare exceptions, the provincial and federal governments chose to allow the MMF and MNC to do pretty much as they pleased with the money as long as they filled out the necessary forms to keep the bureaucrats happy and provided neatly bound financial statements.

During 1979 and 1980, both the federal and provincial governments conducted audits of the MMF. This was during the time when Premier Sterling Lyon had pulled provincial funding, and not long after Employment Minister Lloyd Axworthy lashed out at the MMF for jeopardizing one of his programs. With the exception of the report commissioned by Axworthy (and it dealt only with the MMF's role in that program), none of the audits were ever made public.

Government audits were usually announced after the MMF had once again taken its political battles to the streets and displayed its dirty linen to the public. A federal audit in 1981 did raise "a number of important concerns" that were never revealed, but in typical government fashion, the audits were seldom completed until long after the bad publicity that prompted them died down. Then the audits were shelved and the public refused access to the results. The federal and provincial governments had nothing to gain by looking too closely at MMF operations, as least as long as support for the organization continued to offer political benefits.

That changed with the election of the federal Liberals in 1993. The Liberals didn't have much use for the Métis National Council. The MNC was willing to play ball with whatever party was giving out cheques. They weren't fussy about what colour dress their dance partner was wearing. But Yvon Dumont had spent too much time holding hands with Brian Mulroney for the MNC to be seen as anything but an extension of the Conservative regime.

The Liberals had no compunction about sending in the auditors to investigate how the MNC had spent the $5.8 million the Mulroney Conservatives had given it to spend on the constitution in 1992 and 1993.

The referendum had been run under the Elections Act, and required complete accountability where money had gone. The RCMP were close behind the federal auditors, checking to see if there were grounds for criminal charges to be laid. The government auditors were doing more than just making sure the paperwork matched the bookkeeping and the bank account balanced. They were looking for misuse of funds that were supposed to be used only for constitutional expenses. The auditors didn't think the limousine ordered for the funeral of MNC director Larry Desmeules was a legitimate expense. Nor were the $3,107 in air fares and the $2,500 in per diems the surviving directors paid themselves for attending Desmeules' funeral.

The MNC had gotten a little punch-drunk with all the constitutional money they were given to spend, so they bumped up their per diems to $300 a day. The auditors thought that was just a tad excessive. "We feel that the per diem of $200 is acceptable even though it is generous. Therefore, any per diem claimed over $200 is considered excessive and will not be considered a reasonable and constitutional expense."[2] The auditors calculated the directors had paid themselves an additional $30,800 by bumping up the per diem. The directors and manager also decided to pay themselves each a lump sum of $5,000 to cover any personal expenses that weren't already being covered. The auditor disallowed that $35,000 expense. The auditors also disallowed the $1,500 expense claimed by Gerald Morin to go to Yvon Dumont's swearing in as Lieutenant-Governor. In fact, the auditors found a total of $137,000 in payments made to six MNC directors, two staff members, two consultants and the president of the MNC women's organization were not legitimate expenses. That was on top of the $167,000 the six directors paid themselves to attend regular and special MNC board meetings for the year ending March 31, 1993. In the following eleven months they paid themselves another $102,000. It was all viewed as non-taxable income. The MNC did not issue T-4A slips.

Revenue Canada reassessed the income tax returns for the MNC directors to include the unclaimed income a short time later. Yvon Dumont pleaded ignorance. Breaking the traditional protocol that forbids the Lieutenant-Governor from talking about anything political, he told a CBC-TV reporter, "As far as I know, I was being advised that wasn't something that had to be reported and we weren't going to be T-4'd for it. Since then I've been told things have changed and I can expect to be T-4'd for at least some of that money."[3] Dumont said he would take care of paying the taxes as soon as he got the tax forms.

In the fall of 1994, the MNC was charged by the Commissioner of Canada Elections for "failing to keep track of expenses it incurred while working on behalf of the Yes Canada committee during the 1992 referendum campaign."[4] Executive director Ron Rivard was also facing charges. The MNC promptly fired him.

Governing Themselves

Despite all their problems, the MNC and the MMF were confident they could govern their own Métis nation. The federal and provincial governments had been doling out millions of dollars so the MMF could research how self-government would be accomplished. There was a plan for a Métis nation with land, and a nation without land. The preferred plan called for a land base to be supplied by the government because it would give the Métis nation more legislative authority. It was easier to draw boundaries on a map and call it a nation. Like an Indian reserve, anyone choosing to live on the land would be "subject to the laws of the Métis government by virtue of residence."[5]

The MMF planned to have authority to levy taxes and control natural resources on the land base. They also wanted to assume responsibility for the law enforcement and administration of justice. A Métis nation undefined by land boundaries would be tougher to arrange. The MMF allowed that only those people who chose to participate could be ruled by the Métis nation. Instead of controlling a piece of land, the nation would control people and programs. The nation would also have its own provincial legislative assembly. The provincial organizations working on the Métis Accord, like the MMF, "see their own provincial associations as models for Métis government structures which will promote Métis rights at the provincial level while respecting the autonomy of the Métis at the community and regional levels."[6] They envisioned themselves running an expanded version of the provincial Métis organizations as a fourth level of government, complete with constitutionally entrenched funding and "resource revenue sharing arrangements or equalization and transfer payments from Ottawa. It has also been suggested that in view of the provincial structure of the Métis associations, provincial trust funds could be established from which Métis self-governing institutions at the local, regional and provincial levels could draw funding."[7] The Métis nation would insist on the federal and provincial governments giving over total control in areas it wanted jurisdiction. It would have to be entrenched in the constitution, and there could be no limits on what jurisdictions and institutions the Métis nation could eventually take control.

But was it all just a fantasy dreamed up by the Métis leaders and the governments to keep the grassroots Métis in line during the run up to the Charlottetown referendum? Was it just another version of Stan Fulham's Wizard of Oz, with lots of drama and pageantry about a great Métis nation to disguise how few people the MNC and its provincial organizations really represented? For Ed Schreyer, Métis self-government is nonsense. "It's one thing to talk about a role and function of an organization that starts out as a cultural and social organization that takes on economic efforts. It's another to talk about a local government. A quasi-municipality. I don't think anyone wants Métis self-government. It's rhetoric."[8]

Métis people who want nothing to do with the MMF find the idea of giving the organization legislative authority to be galling. They resent the MMF leaders claiming to speak for them, and most certainly do not want the MMF to have any form of legal power over their lives. Schreyer agrees. "Those who make a declaration and want to join, that's not where the objections are coming from. It's from those who aren't members, and someone who expressly does not want to join has every right to be outraged if this organization tries to control them."[9] The MMF, after all, represents only its own members, just as any cultural, business or recreation club can speak only for its own membership. But the MMF has insisted from the beginning that it speaks for all Métis in Manitoba. They've just never been able to define who that is.

COUNTING THE MÉTIS

Tens of millions of dollars have run through the hands of MMF directors since the organization was created in 1967, but in all those years, there has never been any money to pay for a Métis enumeration. The MMF directors said it was crucial that the Métis be counted, and railed against the government for refusing to give them the money needed.

In 1990, the MNC had the opportunity to participate in the $14 million Post Censal Survey of Native Peoples. Statistics Canada planned to profile all Indian communities with more than 100 people, and to provide that data to a variety of government departments. The MNC could use the same survey to count the Métis in western Canada, if they wanted to buy in. But the MNC said the process was flawed and would not produce valid information on the Métis. The MNC said the Métis were impossible to define anyway. In a report called "Denial by Exclusion: The Métis in Canadian Society," the MNC said, "We defy definitions of race. Our blood can be of many origins. We defy those who want to talk of percentages of this parentage or that. We defy definitions that are based on colour. We come in many hues. We defy cultural definitions for we speak with many tongues and live as part of many cultures. We defy those who would try to (delineate) our citizenship for there are no simple criteria."[10]

The definition of a Métis in the 1989 MMF constitution was "any person who declares himself to be a Métis on account of descent or personal relationship with a family of Métis persons, and who is accepted as a Métis by the Métis community in accordance with the procedures established in this article."[11] Although the constitution didn't spell it out, Indians and Inuit were excluded, and Métis women were included. The definition was amended at the annual assembly in the summer of 1992 (when the secret land claim settlement was still in the works) to restrict membership eligibility to someone who was "a descendant of those Métis who received or were entitled to receive land grants and/or scrip under the provision of the Manitoba Act, 1870, or the Dominion Lands Act..."[12] At the 1994 assembly, that clause was dropped, and "Métis" was simply defined as "an aboriginal person who identifies as Métis and who is distinct from Indian, Inuit or non-Aboriginal."

So, how many Métis are there in Manitoba? Nobody really knows, just as nobody really knows how many Métis lost their land and scrip in the 1880s by fraudulent or illegal means. That will end up being a battle between historians who must ascribe motives to the actions of people who lived more than a hundred years ago. Then it will be up to the government or the courts to decide if compensation should be paid for wrongs done by and to people long dead, and to whom that compensation should be paid.

L'Union Nationale Métisse Saint-Joseph du Manitoba had an alternative to giving compensation to the MNC or the MMF. "Since there were injustices in the past to the Métis," said president Augustine Abraham, we would propose as an alternative that compensation be dealt with by way of a Louis Riel citizenship foundation for the benefit of all Canadians, with some specific benefits for the Métis in the field of education, based on need. This foundation would principally promote the principles and ideals that Riel lived and died for: justice, equality, respect and fraternity for all races and peoples from sea to sea. It would initiate and support the efforts to meet the needs of the less advantaged in our society and deal with the issues that keep us estranged. We could then celebrate our 125th birthday with pride and dignity and hope for the future.[13]

FATAL FLAWS

Between 1965 and 1975, the federal government helped set up hundreds of advocacy groups. As the examples of the MMF and the Manitoba Indian Brotherhood show, there was always a price to be paid for government funding. Politics is the art of compromise, and for some groups, finally gaining access to money to help their cause was worth having to accept some government control. They rationalized that at least something would be done for their cause. But their ability to speak for whatever group or cause they represented had already been compromised. What if the government wanted the group to lie about its members' point of view? How many people would risk destroying their own organization and the jobs it provided by refusing to play the game? The "founding fathers" of the MMF knew the risk they were taking by accepting core funding from government. The rot set in immediately.

For years, people with good intentions and a great deal of naiveté have attempted to fix the MMF. They could see the real poverty in downtown Winnipeg and in remote communities, and they could see the amount of money going to the top of the MMF. But only a few pennies came out the bottom for the needy. They also heard the endless tales of corruption, nepotism, vote-buying, and mismanagement. Surely, if good-hearted people really tried, they said, they could change how the MMF was being run and put all that money in the hands of the poor and marginalized Métis. Couldn't the membership take back control of the MMF?

The membership never had control of the MMF. The locals were created to sign up members to give the organization an appearance of legitimacy. Elections were a necessary evil, but those in power were usually able to exert enough influence over the electorate to ensure the "right" outcome. The same happened at annual assemblies. The delegates to the 1994 assembly spent twenty minutes debating significant amendments to the MMF constitution. The insiders were back in power and the constitution had been amended to make sure that no one could do to Billyjo Delaronde what they had done to Ernie Blais.

The rewritten constitution concentrated power and control in the hands of the MMF president and a judicial tribunal appointed by the president. The president was named the sole spokesperson for the MMF. A new section was added to allow the directors (who renamed themselves "governors") to suspend members for any action considered detrimental to the MMF. There was little room left for members to criticize the existing regime.

But even if the people who wanted to change the MMF had successfully roused the masses to get involved and take control, the new people would have faced exactly the same dilemma faced by the people who first created the MMF. To continue to take the government's money, they'd have to play the game.

CHAPTER TEN

THE GOOD, THE BAD, AND THE UGLY

The MMF has accomplished some good for the Métis people. Poor Métis did get new housing or repairs done to their old homes, but those services were usually heavily weighted towards the family and friends of the directors and program managers. And people did get some help with job training and placement through programs run by the regional offices. But those benefits seemed to have been almost incidental.

MMF directors were well aware of the fact that program cash cows like the property management agreement run through the Housing Branch could just as easily have been run by someone else. They knew that municipalities and government districts could run housing programs at a fraction of the cost, and any of their employment and training programs could just as easily be administered by government bureaucrats.

In the Conservative government's final budget in the spring of 1993, some CMHC housing programs were cut. Brian Mulroney had taken care of Yvon Dumont. He no longer needed to take care of the Métis groups by protecting their programs. Since those were the same housing programs providing such large prfits to the MMF and other provincial Métis groups, there was a mad scramble to get replacement programs in place.

The Métis National Council was negotiating with CMHC on behalf of the provincial groups, but it had competition. The Native Council of Canada had put in a proposal of its own. A coalition including the Canadian Housing and Renewal Association and the Canadian Association of Municipalities was lobbying to take over the housing programs, too. The MNC was invited to a meeting of the Social Housing Coalition in Toronto to talk about new program ideas. Director Ron Swain was representing the MNC at the meeting. "But don't blow our plan," the other directors warned Swain, "because they may want to beat us to the punch. Hold our cards close to our chests because they are our competitors."[1] CMHC bureaucrats came through for the MNC. The Manitoba Métis Federation now benefits from the surplus of a new housing program.

When asked what the MMF has done for them, some Métis people credit the MMF with helping to create Métis pride by giving the Métis a presence on the national political stage, and by creating a greater public awareness of Métis history and issues. Métis people are proud of the fact that a Métis has been appointed lieutenant-governor of Manitoba, regardless of their personal feelings about Dumont or how he got there. But after that, people quickly run out of good things to say about the MMF.

The MMF's role as an organization battling government to better the lives of the Métis has, since the beginning, been little more than an illusion. Smoke and mirrors. Wind and rabbit tracks.

When Billyjo Delaronde made his first appearance at a news conference as the new MMF president, he was asked if he was worried about the credibility of an organization continually dogged by accusations of fraud and corruption. With a half-smile, he shrugged and said, "That's how politics is done." Sadly, it appears he's right.

END NOTES

Chapter One: The Glory Days

1. *Winnipeg Free Press*, June 2, 1990.
2. Report of the Métis Senate Commission, Round One, July, 1991.
3. Report of the Manitoba Métis Senate Commission, *National Unity and Constituional Reform*, p. 74.
4. Ibid., p. 22.
5. Minutes of the Manitoba Métis Federation Land Claims Committee, August 9, 1992.
6. Ibid.
7. Ibid.
8. Ibid.
9. Minutes of the Manitoba Métis Federation board meeting, July 28-29, 1992.
10. Letter, Augstine Abraham to Joe Clark, Constitutional Affairs Minister, et al, June 29, 1992.

Chapter Two: The Bubble Burst

1. Clark, Joe. *A Nation Too Good to Lose*, p. 119.
2. *The Globe & Mail*, October 30, 1992.
3. *Winnipeg Free Press*, November 17, 1992.
4. Ibid., January 23, 1993.

Chapter Three: In the Beginning

1. MacEwan, Grant. *Métis Makers of History*, p. 3.
2. Ibid., p. 2.
3. Sealey, B. and Antoinne Lussier. *The Métis, Canada's Forgotten People*, p. 5.
4. Ibid.
5. Cockran, Rev. W. Church Missionary Archives, correspondence, 1833.
6. MacEwan, p. 4.
7. Ibid., p. 2.
8. Ross, Alexander. *The Red River Settlement*, excerpts.
9. Flanagan, Thomas. *Métis Lands in Manitoba*, p. 14.
10. Harrison, Julian. *Métis, People Between Two Worlds*, p. 75.

11. Zeilig, Ken. *Ste. Madeline*, "An Interview with Thomas Berger," p. 196.
12. Parliamentary debate on the Manitoba Act, *Parliamentary Debates*, extracts, 1870.
13. Translation of Rîchot's speech of June 24, 1870 to the Legislative Assemby of Assiniboia, "The New Nation", 1870.
14. Flanagan, p. 42.
15. Ibid., p. 94.
16. Ibid., p. 232.
17. Report of the Debates of the House of Commons, July 16, 1885.
18. Harrison, p. 57.
19. *Royal Commission Report of the Condition of the Halfbreed Population in Alberta*, 1935, p. 14.
20. Sealey, p. 9.

Chapter Four: The Métis, Rediscovered

1. As according to Stan Fulham.
2. Burke, James. *Paper Tomahawks*, p. 49.
3. Lussier, Antoine and Sealey, *Métis, The Other Natives*, pp. 157-58.
4. Author's interview with Stan Fulham.
5. Ibid.
6. Ibid.
7. Ibid.
8. Ibid.
9. Ibid.
10. *Winnipeg Free Press*, July 22, 1976.
11. Ibid., April 11, 1979.
12. Ibid., April 16, 1979.
13. Burke, p. 10.
14. Author's interview with Jean Allard.
15. *Winnipeg Free Press*, July 3, 1979.
16. Ibid, August 10, 1979.
17. *Brandon Sun*, March 11, 1979.
18. *Winnipeg Tribune*, June 6, 1980.
19. Ibid.
20. *Winnipeg Free Press*, June 9, 1980.
21. Ibid, September 1, 1980.
22. *Winnipeg Free Press*, August 11, 1980.

Chapter Five: The Dumont Dynasty

1. Manitoba Dept. of Justice, Aboriginal Justice Inquiry, Community Hearing Transcripts, 552, 553, excerpts.
2. Ibid.
3. *Winnipeg Free Press*, August 30, 1971.
4. Ibid, May 12, 1984.
5. Ibid.
6. Ibid., June 18, 1984.

7. *Le Métis*, (a tabloid newspaper produced intermitently by the Manitoba Métis Federation) Centennial Assembly Edition, 1985.

Chapter Six: More Money

1. Memorandum, Yvon Dumont to all MMF directors, vice-presidents and staff, August 4, 1992.
2. Minutes, Manitoba Métis Federation Committee Meeting, December 17-18, 1991.
3. *Winnipeg Free Press*, January 9, 1986.
4. MMF Interim Management Audit Report, April 16, 1993.
5. Ibid.
6. *Le Métis*, February 1, 1986. Author's italics.
7. MMF Housing Branch, Program Plan–Interim Submission, December 17, 1991.
8. Métis Self-government Tripartitie Negotiations, Annual Report 1992, excerpts.
9. *Winnipeg Free Press*, July 2, 1992.
10. 2381576 Manitoba Ltd., Financial Statement, 1991.
11. Interlake Métis Association Inc., Financial Statements, 1992 and 1993.
12. *Stonewall Argus*, January 29, 1992.
13. MMCII, Notes to Financial Statements, March 31, 1992.
14. Author 's interivew with Ernie Blais.

Chapter Seven: Just Say Yes

1. Author's interview with Louise Newans.
2. *Ottawa Citizen*, March 26, 1992.
3. Letter, Mary Weigers, NMAC president to Gayle Stacey-Moore, NWAC, March 24, 1992.
4. Métis Council of Women, press release, September 16, 1992.
5. Letter, Sheila Genaille, NMCW president to Sandra Delaronde, NWOM president, September 18, 1992.

Chapter Eight: A Poison Pill

1. Memo, Yvon Dumont, MMF president to Debbie Sinclair, MMF finance offficer, February 3, 1993
2. Memo, Laura Guiboche, MMF personnel director to Ed Swain, February 3, 1993.
3. *Winnipeg Free Press*, April 15, 1993.
4. Ibid.
5. Author's interview with Ernie Blais.
6. Ibid.
7. *Winnipeg Free Press*, July 31, 1993.
8. The Court of Queen's Bench of Manitoba, CI-93-01-76809, excerpt.
9. Ibid, November 4, 1994.
10. Author's interiview with Lesia Szwaluk.
11. Ibid.
12. Ibid.
13. Ibid.

14. Letter, Darren Praznik, Manitoba minister of Northern Affairs to MMF Interim Board of Directors, February 2, 1994, excerpt.
15. Deloitte & Touche, Summary of Audit Engagements for MMF, June 23, 1994.
16. The Court of Queen's Bench of Manitoba, Cl-94-01-78622, March 16, 1994.
17. Ibid.
18. Ibid.
19. Author's interview with Lesia Szwaluk.
20. Ibid.
21. *Winnipeg Free Press*, July 23, 1994.
22. The Court of Queen's Bench of Manitoba, Cl-93-01-76809, November 4, 1994.
23. Ibid.

Chapter Nine: Betrayed

1. Letter, Augustine Abraham to Joe Clark, June 29, 1992.
2. Review of Métis National Council, Department of Candian Heritage, March 11, 1994.
3. CBWT-TV, *24-Hours*, April 27, 1994.
4. *Winnipeg Free Press*, November 3, 1994.
5. Métis National Council, *The Métis Nation's Parallel Process*, 1992, p. 25.
6. Ibid.
7. Ibid. p. 26.
8. Author's interview with Ed Schreyer.
9. Ibid.
10. Métis National Council, "Denial by Exclusion: The Métis in Canadian Society", essay presented at MNC Annual Assembly, 1991, p. 170.
11. MMF Constitution, ratified at 21st Assembly, 1989, Article III 1 (a).
12. Ibid., ratified at MMF Annual Assembly, 1992, Article III 1 (b).
13. Letter, Augustine Abraham to Joe Clark, Constitutional Affairs minister, June 29, 1992.

Chapter Ten: The Good, the Bad, and the Ugly

1. Minutes from the Métis National Council teleconference call, June 2, 1993.

INDEX

Sheila Jones Morrison, a former newspaper editor, has written and appeared on such shows as CBC's *Morningside, Radio Noon* and CBC TV's *Newsworld*. She was nominated for the Canadian Association of Journalists' Outstanding Investigative Journalism Awards in 1991. Ms Jones Morrison currently reports and serves as desk editor for CBC Radio News. She and her two daughters live in the country north of Winnipeg, Manitoba.